# CHAUCER
*and his world*

Althogh his life queynte be · the resemblance

Of hym · hath in me oo fressh liknesse

That to putte other men · in remembrance

Of his psone · I haue here the liknesse

Do make · to this ende in sothefastnesse

That they that haue of hym · lost thoght and mynde

By this peynture · may ageyn hym fynde


The ymages that in the chirches ben

Maken folk thynke · on god and on his seyntes

Whan they the ymages · beholden and seen

Where as vnsight of hem causeth restreyntes

Of thoghtes goode · whan a thyng depeynt is

Or entitiled · if men taken of it hede

Thoght of the liknesse · it wole in hem brede


Yit som holden oppynyon and sey

That none ymages · schuld y maked be

They erren foule · and goon out of the wey

Of trouthe · han they skant sensibilitee

Passe ouer now · that blissed trinitee

Vpon my maisters soule · mercy haue

ffor hym lady eke · thy mercy I craue


Moore other thyng wold · I fayne speke and touche

Heere in this booke · but such is my dulnesse

ffor that all voide · and empty is my pouche

That all my lust · is queynt with heuynesse

An heuy sprite · comaundeth stilnesse

And haue I spoke of pees · I schall be stille

God sende vs pees · yf it be his wille

# CHAUCER
## and his world

BY F. E. HALLIDAY

A STUDIO BOOK

THE VIKING PRESS · NEW YORK

# PREFACE

As Chaucer was throughout his career a royal and government servant, many facts about him exist in contemporary records, and it is fairly easy to trace the general outline of his life. It is not always easy, however, to say exactly when he wrote his poems, and I have worked them into my narrative at the periods when they seem most likely to have been written. Even the order of the telling of *The Canterbury Tales* is uncertain in places, but Skeat's arrangement seems to me acceptable, and this I have adopted.

In quotation I have modernized much of the spelling, for two reasons. First to make the verse easy to read; and for the same reason I have very occasionally substituted a modern for an archaic word. The manuscripts from which the poems are printed are those of fifteenth-century scribes; the spelling, therefore, is not necessarily Chaucer's, and such a line as, 'To take oure wey ther as I yow devyse', may just as well be written, 'To take our way there as I you devise'. Secondly: to avoid the effect of quaintness and naïveté that the old spelling is apt to give the modern reader, for Chaucer was neither quaint nor naïve. I have, of course, retained the final *e* of a word where it is necessary to the scansion of the verse.

The following very rough guide to Chaucer's language and pronunciation may be helpful:

Old English was the highly inflected Teutonic language of the Anglo-Saxons, in which, as in modern German, nouns and adjectives had different endings to distinguish number, gender and case.

Middle English was that of the Middle Ages, *c.* 1150–1500, when, after the Norman Conquest, a number of French words were incorporated, and many of the old inflections dropped.

There were five main dialects, the East Midland being that spoken in London and by Chaucer.

ACCENT
In words of French origin, the stress is generally at the end: (*viságe*, *labóur*, *doctríne*).

SHORT VOWELS
As in modern English.
*u* (often spelled *o*) as in *pull*: (*yonge sonne*).

LONG VOWELS
*a*, as in *father*: (*bathe, make*).
*e, ee* (modern *ee* or *ie*), as *a* in *late*: (*sleep, thief*).
   (modern *e* or *ea*), as in *there*: (*were, breath*).
*i, y*, as in *machine*: (*ride, thy*).
*o, oo* (modern *oo*), as in *nose*: (*good, book*).
   (modern *o, oa, oe*), as in *broad*: (*go, roast, foe*).
*u, ou, ow*, as in *root*: (*flour, now*).

DIPHTHONGS
Mainly as in modern English, but
*au* as *ou* in *house*; cf. German, *Haus*: (*cause, Chaucer*).

CONSONANTS
Mostly as in modern English, and all pronounced distinctly:
*fol-k, g-nawe, son-ne.*
*gh* as *ch* in *loch*: thus *knight* is *k-nicht* (German, *Knecht*).
Initial *th* as in *thin*.
Final *s*, as *s*, not *z*.

FINAL *e*
Lightly pronounced, as *a* in *sofa*. It is always pronounced, even at the end of a
line, except in some common words like *were, these*, and before a word beginning with a vowel, or with a silent or unemphatic *h*: *honour, he, his, hath*.
An *e* in the middle of a word is sometimes a distinct syllable: *tru-e-ly, neigh-e-
bour.*
Final *ed, en, es* are generally distinctly pronounced:

> *A Knight ther(e) was, and that a worthy man,*
> *That from the timé that he first began*
> *To riden out, he lovéd chivalryé,*
> *Truth(e) and honour, freedom and courtesyé.*

   If this guide is too elaborate, some idea of Middle English may be obtained
by pronouncing vowels as in modern French. And, of course, Chaucer's
poetry can be enjoyed simply by reading it as modern English, though the final
*e* must be pronounced to preserve the metre. For two excellent recordings of
Chaucer read in Middle English, see Bibliography, p. 129.

   There is a short glossary on page 132.

St Ives
Cornwall

F.E.H.

*In grateful memory*
*of*
WALTER NEURATH

Medieval London, from St Paul's to Thames Street, where Chaucer was probably born and spent his early years.

NEARLY A HUNDRED YEARS after the death of Chaucer, the first printer of his works, Caxton, described him, with uncharacteristic floridity, as 'the worshipful father and first founder and embellisher of ornate eloquence in our English'. Another two hundred years, and Dryden styled him 'the father of English poetry'. But Dryden did not understand the pronunciation of medieval English, and had to confess that 'the verse of Chaucer is not harmonious to us.' 'Yet,' he added, 'they who lived with him . . . thought it musical.' Indeed they did, and probably no English poet has been more honoured by his contemporaries. Gower, the older poet, claimed him as his disciple, and called on others to 'greet well Chaucer'; for Lydgate, a younger man, he was 'My master Chaucer . . . chief poet of Bretayne', as also for Hoccleve, who had his portrait painted in the margin of one of the poems in which he paid tribute to 'The firste finder of our fair langage'. Nor was his fame limited to England, for Eustache Deschamps wrote a *ballade* to celebrate the 'Grand translateur, noble Geffroy Chaucier'.

The name Chaucer is derived from the Old French *chaucier*, a cordwainer, or shoemaker, and there had long been Chaucers living in London in the ward of Cordwainer Street. The family seems to have come from East Anglia, and Geoffrey's grandfather, Robert, one of the collectors of customs upon wine in the Port of London, owned a small property in Ipswich. He died *c.* 1316, and the house would have been inherited by his son John when he came of age, but John's aunt Agnes, who lived in Ipswich, was anxious to preserve it in her branch of the family. In 1324, therefore, when John was only twelve, she planned his abduction from London, 'by force and arms', and his marriage with her daughter. The plot failed: John was rescued, and brought up in London by his mother and stepfather; for the widow had married again, another Chaucer, Richard, possibly a cousin of her former husband.

Like Robert, Richard was in the wine trade, a prosperous vintner, or importer of wines, who introduced his stepson to the business. When John was about twenty, in the early 1330s, he married a widow, Agnes Northwell, niece

and heiress of Hamo de Copton, a wealthy citizen of London who owned property in Aldgate and a house in Thames Street, and it was probably in this house, between London Bridge and St Paul's Cathedral, that Geoffrey, son of John and Agnes Chaucer, was born in, or soon after, 1340.

If he was born in 1340, it was in the same year that one of the many, too many, sons of Edward III and his Queen, Philippa of Hainault, was born in Ghent: John, called after the anglicized form of his Flemish birthplace, John of Gaunt. Edward III was twenty-eight, and already had two sons, Edward, Prince of Wales and first Duke of Cornwall, who was to become better known as the Black Prince; and Lionel, later Earl of Ulster and Duke of Clarence.

The London of 1340 was much the biggest town in England, a city of some 40,000 inhabitants. Most of them were crowded within the walls, which ran in a semi-circle from the Fleet river on the west to the Tower on the east, though suburbs were already beginning to spring up beyond them. The streets were narrow, the houses mostly of timber and thatch, above which rose the towers of

(*above, left*) Medieval grape-harvest.

(*above*) The fourteenth-century wine trade.
  'Now keep you from the white and from the red,
  And namely from the white wine of Lepe,
  That is to sell in Fish Street or in Cheap.'

(*left*) Deed, witnessed by John Chaucer, whereby Edmund de Sutton granted John de Stodeye the Vintry Estates in London.

Seal of Edward III, 1340-72.

Medieval sheep-shearing. Wool was England's most important export, though cloth was beginning to overtake it.

Seal die: Mayoralty of the Wool-Staple, Westminster.

a hundred churches and the great wooden spire of St Paul's Cathedral. It was the business and financial centre, and chief port of England, a city of merchants, bankers, shopkeepers, clerks, craftsmen and apprentices.

It was crossed from west to east, Newgate to Aldgate, by West Cheap and Cornhill, along which rumbled wagons bringing the wool of the West Country and grain of East Anglia; from north to south, Bishopsgate to London Bridge, by the road that brought the wool of the Yorkshire abbeys and food of the southern counties. London Bridge with its twenty arches, itself a street of shops and houses connecting the City with the suburb of Southwark on the south bank, was one of the sights of Europe, and here was the Port of London, into which came the cloths of Flanders and wines of France, and from which was shipped England's staple product, wool.

London Bridge: a street with a church. On the tower commanding the drawbridge, traitors' heads were exposed on pikes.

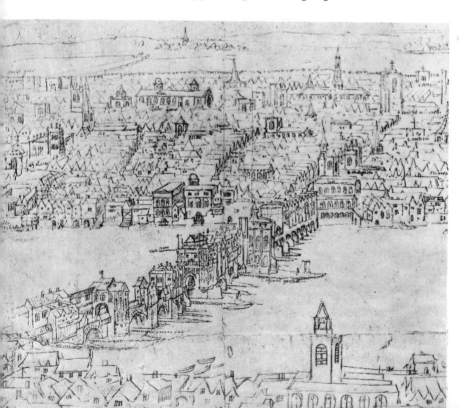

London: from the Augustinian Priory of St Mary Overy of Southwark to St Paul's in the City on the north bank of the Thames. ▶

Medieval justice: the
Court of King's Bench.

The government of London was in the hands of wealthy merchants, and the walled City is to be distinguished from aristocratic Westminster two miles further up the river. Here was the Abbey, rebuilt in the former century in the early Gothic style, and the Palace, not only a royal residence, but the seat of government, where Parliament met, while the great Hall of William Rufus was the home of the newly developing law courts. Here the lawyers worked, but between Westminster and London they had recently built lodgings (similar to the newly erected colleges of Oxford and Cambridge), Inns of Court, such as the Inner and Middle Temple.

A mason and a carpenter being
examined by a Gild Warden before
being admitted master craftsmen.

The Londoners were freemen, as were the inhabitants of most other towns,
and each local craft was organized as a gild of master craftsmen, the officers of
which fixed wages, prices and conditions of work. Most countrymen, however,
were serfs on the estate of a lord of the manor, tenants who were leased a few
acres to farm in return for working on their lord's domain. Their freedom was
limited, for they were bound to the soil, forbidden to leave the manor without
their lord's consent. New movements were afoot, however, and this medieval
organization of gild and manor was to be severely strained during the sixty years
of Chaucer's lifetime.

13

Border of a fourteenth-century illuminated psalter.

A canopied tomb in the Decorated style: the Percy shrine, Beverley Minster, Yorkshire. ▶

The thirteenth century had been a period of religious fervour, even of asceticism, but in the fourteenth there was a decline of spiritual values as wealth and luxury increased. This new extravagance can be seen in its art. In architecture the severe, functional early Gothic relaxed and burgeoned into the flowing curves and ogival elaborations of the Decorated style. Effigies on tombs lay half concealed under towering canopies, and in stained glass the willowy figures of saints and soldiers were dwarfed by similar fantastic structures. The art of illumination, of illustrating manuscripts, for there were no printed books, underwent a corresponding elaboration, saints and martyrs giving place to a riot of worldly and realistic ornament: birds, beasts, hunting-scenes, knights, ladies and heraldic shields. And the costumes of these knights and ladies became more and more ostentatiously extravagant as the century advanced.

The influence of France on English culture was predominant, for in 1340 French was still the language of the upper classes, as it had been since the Norman Conquest. Latin was the language of lawyers and the Church, and Middle English, halfway between Anglo-Saxon and our modern tongue, was, in a variety of dialects, the speech of illiterate serfs and the common people. There was little to encourage the writing of English, and the verse romances and lyrics of the period, some of them very beautiful, were mainly inspired by French models. About 1320, however, came a long history of the world, *Cursor Mundi*, written in octosyllabic couplets of the northern dialect. The author explains that he has written the book

> *For the love of English folk,*
> *English folk of merry England,*
> *For the common to understand.*
> *Frenche rhymes hear I read*
> *Commonly in every stead;*
> *Most is writ for Frenche man,*
> *But what for him that no French can?*

14

It is significant and important, for the poem is full of Bible stories that served as material for the religious plays that unknown authors began to write in English at about this time, culminating in the great northern cycles of Chester, York, Coventry and Wakefield about 1370, when Chaucer was beginning to write.

Like many fourteenth-century poets, the author of *Cursor Mundi* attacks the vices of his age:

> *In riot and in rigolage*
> *Spend many both their youth and age,*
> *For now no one is held in course ·*
> *But he that loveth paramours.*

There was some truth in the charge. The revival of interest in the legendary adventures of Arthur, Charlemagne, Roland and other paladins and princes had encouraged a cult of knight-errantry and courtly love, according to which, as Launcelot had his Guinevere, Tristram his Iseult, so every knight should have a mistress, serving her humbly, devotedly, in return for her favours. This romantic, idealized conception of love, whatever its origin, had been developed among the aristocracy of southern France in the eleventh and twelfth centuries, when countless love songs were written: roundels, ballades, virelays, such as Chaucer himself was to write in his youth. At best this led to good manners and a code of courtesy among the upper classes, but it also led to insincerity, affectation and a bogus chivalry: a captured knight was spared for his ransom, but a common soldier had his throat slit like a pig.

COURTLY LOVE

◀ 'The life so short, the craft so long to learne,
Th'assay so hard, so sharp the conqueringe,
The dreadful joy that alway slip so yerne,
All this mean I by love.'

*(left below)*
'Full oft I of myself divine
That I am true Tristam the secounde.'

An ivory casket representing the popular romance of Tristram and Iseult.

Joust and capture of the Castle of Love.

Gold noble of Edward III, 1360-69.

Fourteenth-century English jug with fleur-de-lis.

Edward III was a principal devotee of chivalry. To preserve the Flemish market for English wool, and the wine exports from the English province of Guienne, both threatened by the French, he put forward a preposterous claim to the throne of France, quartered her lilies with the lions of England on his shield, and invaded the country. In 1346 he destroyed Barfleur, devastated the Normandy coast, won a dazzling victory at Crécy, and captured Calais. To celebrate the campaign there were tournaments and feasts, and at Windsor, probably in the spring of 1348, King Edward emulated the glories of King Arthur in another Fellowship of the Round Table, by instituting the Order of

Sir Geoffrey Luttrell: an English knight at the beginning of the Hundred Years War.

Edward III in Robes of the Order of the Garter, with 'France Ancient' (fleurs-de-lis) quartered with the lions of England. ▶

The Black Death. Burning infected clothes.

the Garter. A few weeks later the plague that had swept through Europe crossed the Channel into Dorset, and by November it was in London.

In the course of the catastrophic year 1348–9 the Black Death killed almost half the people of England – Richard Chaucer was one of its victims – reducing its number from some four million to little more than two million. As a result, there was not enough labour to cultivate the land, serfs demanded their freedom or ran away from the manor, prices rose, and free labourers, in both country and

Looting.

Archery practice. The new English technique: leaning the body into the bow.

'Out goon the swordes as
            the silver brighte;
The helmes they to-hewen
            and to-shrede.' ▶

town, demanded higher wages. Their masters in Parliament replied with statutes to preserve the old order, to enforce serfdom and keep down wages – measures that led to great bitterness and unrest, to strikes and a bloody revolt thirty years later.

The beginning of the Hundred Years War and scourge of the Black Death coincided with the early years of Geoffrey Chaucer. He was one of the lucky ones, and probably escaped the plague because in 1348 he was in Southampton, where his father was Deputy to the King's Butler. He would be about ten when he returned to London and his home in Thames Street. There he would hear French, of a sort, spoken as much as English, and when his formal education began it would be French that he was taught to read. We do not know where he went to school, but he may have gone to the school attached to St Paul's Cathedral, near his home, where he would learn Latin grammar, logic and rhetoric, the art of speaking and writing, and be introduced to the Latin classics, notably to Ovid, his favourite author. How long he continued with a school education is unknown, but we learn from the Household Accounts of Elizabeth, Countess of Ulster, that in April 1357 he was in her service, and supplied with a new suit of clothes: a paltok, or short cloak, a pair of red and

ment le cōmorune gent. checon leia agtreaunier uou       dir aunte ocrue p le auer. pi met
c. Cou est dimt nouf esimome leen ō le iour de droir inoumer for       met abroche.

'To 1 paltok for Galfrido Chaucer iiii s.' The first reference to Chaucer, as a Page in the household of the Countess of Ulster.

black breeches, and a pair of shoes. The outfit cost 7s, or, since the value of money was then about fifty times greater than today, £17 (about $40).

Elizabeth, only child of the Earl of Ulster, had inherited his great estates on his death, and, brought up by Queen Philippa and Edward III in the English Court, was betrothed to their son Lionel, whom she married when she was about twelve. In 1357 she was twenty-five, eight years older than Chaucer, and six years older than her husband. At this time the young couple and their miniature court were in London, preparing for the festivities at Windsor Castle on St George's Day, which would account for Chaucer's new clothes. As transport of food was difficult, royalty, like the nobility and gentry, moved from manor to manor, consuming supplies in rotation. In May they were at Woodstock near Oxford, where more clothes were bought for Chaucer, and in December they were in Yorkshire, at their principal manor of Hatfield near Doncaster. Here they spent Christmas, and Chaucer received 2s 6d 'for necessaries against the Feast of the Nativity'. Among the guests was John of Gaunt, Lionel's younger brother, a boy of the same age as Chaucer, and it seems probable that here a friendship began.

We can do little more than guess how and when Geoffrey entered the service of the Earl and Countess of Ulster. However, his father was a prosperous man, perhaps with some pretensions to gentility, and he had connections with the

'At this time it pleased the King to rebuild the Castle of Windsor, which was begun by King Arthur. Then King Edward determined to make an order of Knights of the Blue Garter; and a feast to be held yearly, on St George's Day, at Windsor.' Froissart.

Court. In some capacity or other, probably as an experienced vintner, he had accompanied Edward III to Flanders on one of the opening campaigns of the French war, and had served as his Deputy Butler. Moreover, his wife Agnes was an heiress, and by her previous marriage related to officials at Court. Geoffrey's parents had some influence and, if they also had ambitions for their son, might well have secured his acceptance as a page in the Ulster household, possibly when he was about twelve.

His education would not be neglected, but the emphasis would now be on courtly behaviour. Under the charge of a Master of Henchmen, pages learned all about horses and chivalry: the ceremonies of hunt, hawking and tourna, ment, and how to ride and wear their equipment. They were also taught more cultural accomplishments: to dance, sing and play the harp and pipe, and to speak and read other languages, a useful training for a future diplomat and poet.

In 1357 Chaucer was seventeen, and in the early spring of 1358 we can imagine him riding in Hatfield Chase, like the young squire whom he was to describe in *The Canterbury Tales*:

> *Embroidered was he, as it were a meede*
> *All full of freshe flowres, white and reede.*
> *Singing he was, or fluting all the day;*
> *He was as fresh as is the month of May.*

23

Perhaps he was already 'making' love songs like the squire, for he tells us that while he was young he wrote 'ballades, roundels, virelays' in honour of Love, no doubt in French. They have been lost, but almost certainly he had learned the courtesy that was always to distinguish him as a poet.

The Hundred Years War had flared up again in 1355, when the Black Prince and his chivalry devastated southern France from sea to sea. In the next

(*above left*) Pages, or valets, helping to dress their master before a fire. The fireplace was a new luxury.

(*above*) Waiting at table, playing the harp.

(*right*) 'A baggepipe well could he blow and sound.'

(*left*) Knights riding through London to a tournament.

'He coulde hunt at wilde deer,
And ride an hawking for riveer,
With grey goshawk on hande.'

year he repeated his exploits in central France, and at Poitiers won a victory even more dazzling than that at Crécy ten years before. Among his prisoners was the French King John, a prize to be carefully preserved and treated with every courtesy, for his ransom was set at three million gold crowns.

Then, in November 1359, King Edward himself invaded northern France, advancing on Rheims, where he hoped to force the French to crown him as their king. He was accompanied by his four eldest sons and, according to the great historian of the age, Froissart, 'There was not knight, squire or man of honour, from the age of twenty to sixty years, that did not go.' Chaucer, nearly twenty, was there, among the retinue of Prince Lionel. It was a savage campaign in atrocious weather, finishing in the following April with the desolation of the country round Paris, and an unsuccessful siege. Chaucer missed the worst, for he was taken prisoner early in the campaign at 'Retters', probably Rethel, near Rheims. However, in March 1360 he was freed, Edward III contributing £16, about £800 today, towards his ransom. He paid rather more towards the restoration of a horse; but in the age of chivalry horses were more important than boys, and presumably Prince Lionel paid something towards the release of his servant.

In May preliminaries of peace were arranged at Brétigny, Edward III receiving most of south-west France in full sovereignty, in return for renouncing his claim to the French throne. King John was taken to Calais, where he was confined until the first instalment of his ransom had been paid, and the treaty ratified. Prince Lionel was there, and Chaucer had his first experience in diplomacy when he carried letters between Calais and London. John was freed in October, and Edward returned to England to celebrate his triumphs. It was the high-water mark of his reign, and the tide of success began to recede.

Chaucer's connection with the Ulster household did not last much longer; when Lionel went to Ireland as its Governor in 1361, it seems unlikely that Chaucer went with him, for he makes no mention of Ireland in his works. The Countess died in 1363, and it was probably at about this time that he entered the service of the King, and, if a late-sixteenth-century report is to be credited, studied at the Inner Temple. It was not unusual for the King's servants to train at the Inns of Court for what we should today call the Civil Service, perhaps not unusual to beat a friar in Fleet Street, as Chaucer is said to have done, a most unchaucerian proceeding, for which he was fined two shillings. Certainly he was in the King's service in 1367, when Edward III awarded his 'dilectus vallectus', his beloved valet, Geoffrey Chaucer, a life annuity of twenty marks or, a mark being 13s 4d, £13.6.8.

By this time his father had died, his mother had married again, and he himself was married. Evidently the romance had begun in the royal household, for

King John of France surrenders to the Black Prince after the Battle of Poitiers, 1356.

Restormel Castle, the headquarters of the Black Prince as Duke of Cornwall.

King John of France in captivity.

(*left*) Lionel, Duke of Clarence: Chaucer's first master.

(*right*) Rheims Cathedral, where the kings of France were crowned.
It was near Rheims that Chaucer was captured on the French
campaign of 1359.

Edward III grants the Black Prince the Principality of Aquitaine.

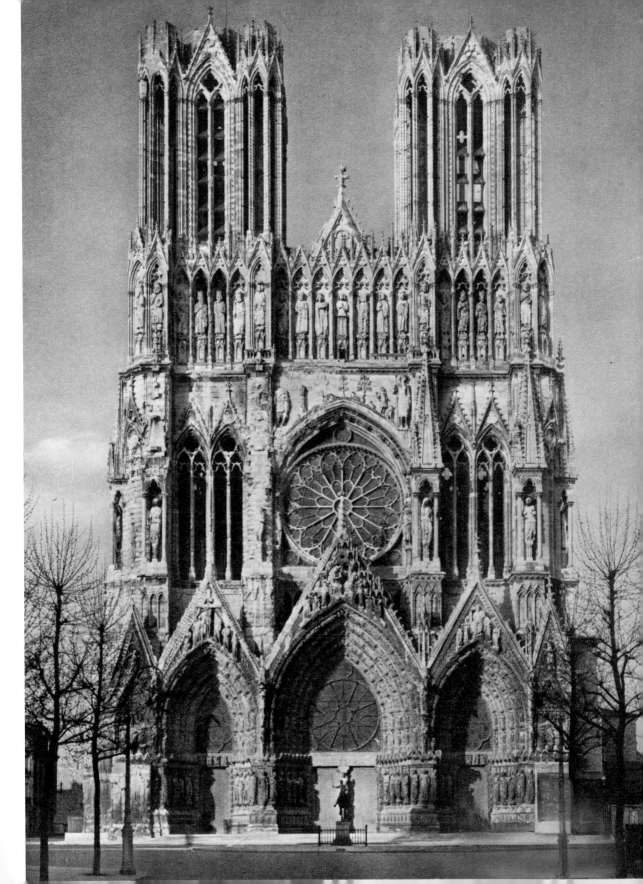

Calais, an English possession, where exported wool was taxed and sold.

his wife was a lady-in-waiting to Queen Philippa, from whom in 1366 she received the first payment of her salary of ten marks. Her name was also Philippa: Philippa de Roet, daughter of a Flemish knight, whose other daughter, Katherine, was also married to an Englishman, Sir Hugh Swynford.
• It was an advantageous alliance for the vintner's son, but he had another asset besides a wife of gentle birth: he was a poet, and the 'many a song and many a lecherous lay' that he had written must have made him one of the most

Edward III grants his 'beloved valet Galfridus Chaucer' an annuity of twenty marks, 20 June 1367.

popular members of the Court of Edward III. Now that he was a married man, however, he set to work on something that would be more acceptable to Philippa, and no less popular at Court.

His visits to France would have been an inspiration to the impressionable young man, and it may have been during the few months of his captivity that he read, or re-read, the most influential of all French poems, and conceived the idea of translating it into English. This was *Le Roman de la Rose*, begun by Guillaume de Lorris about 1225, and completed some forty years later by Jean de Meun. As begun by Lorris, the poem is a medieval version of Ovid's *Art of Love*, a romantic allegory within a world of dream, in which the sleeper is taught 'the craft of love', the courtly make-believe of the period. Meun, however, was a very different character: a young, middle-class scholar, who added thousands of lines of erudition, realism and anti-romantic matter.

In his translation, *The Romaunt of the Rose*, Chaucer adopts the octosyllabic couplets of the original, and follows Lorris very closely, almost line by line. The young Dreamer discovers a garden guarded by a wall on which are portrayed uncourtly qualities that are excluded: Hate, for example:

> *Y-frounced foul was hir visage,*
> *And grenning for despitous rage;*
> *Hir nose snorted up for teen.*

'My lady cometh.'

Inside it is very different, and when the courteous maiden Idleness opens the gate for him, he hears birds singing their lays of love as sweet and clear as those of mermaids. Here Chaucer allows himself a gloss:

> *Though we mermaidens clepe them here*
> *In English, as is our usaunce,*
> *Men clepen them sireyns in Fraunce.*

In the garden the Dreamer finds Sir Mirth and a company of beautiful ladies, one of whom, Courtesy, invites him to join their dance. He then wanders among the trees to a well, with the legend: 'Here starf the faire Narcisus', and in the leisurely medieval manner he interpolates Ovid's story of the Death of Narcissus. At the bottom of this Well of Love is the Mirror Perilous, into which anyone who looks will see something that will 'lead him into loving'. He sees a rose-bush, traces it by its scent, and chooses a bud

> *So fair, that of the remnaunt none*
> *Ne prized I half so well as it . . .*
> *The swote smelle sprong so wide*
> *That it did all the place aboute —*

31

Here, in the middle of a couplet, Chaucer breaks off, and apparently it was left mainly to others to continue the translation: how the Dreamer becomes Love's servant, and is introduced to the art of love. He must serve and praise all women, always be courteous and cheerful, avoid ribaldry and pride, sing and play, dance and joust, wear fashionable clothes with flowers in his hat, have at least two pairs of shoes and, like a royal page or valet,

> *Thine hondis wash, thy teeth make white,*
> *And let no filth upon thee be;*
> *Thy nailes black if thou mayst see,*
> *Void it away deliverly,*
> *And comb thine head right jollily.*

In *The Legend of Good Women*, written twenty years later, the God of Love accuses Chaucer of having translated the 'heretical' *Romaunt of the Rose*, which must mean that he had translated at least some of Meun's addition, for nothing could be more orthodox than Lorris's part. But for Chaucer writing was a spare-time occupation, and there were more important things to do; the poem was too long, and he did not finish it. Yet his fragment was an invaluable exercise in description and narrative, in the making of metrical couplets in English, and he was never to forget what he learned from his study of Lorris and Meun, the dreamy idealism and lucid style of the one, the earthy realism and irony of the other, and his later works are full of echoes from *Le Roman de la Rose*.

'I wente soone
To bed, as I was wont to done
And fast I sleep; and in sleeping . . .'

'I saw a garden right anon,
Full long and broad, and everydel
Enclosed it was, and walled well.' ▶

There were other things that could account for his abandoning his translation. By this time he was an esquire, and the days of menial service as page and valet were over: running errands, holding torches, making beds, brushing clothes and laying tables. He was now to be tried in diplomacy, and in 1368 was sent abroad on the King's business, with £10 for his expenses. Men of Chaucer's calibre were needed now. Edward III's Fellowship of the Round Table was breaking up. In 1367 the Black Prince, Governor of Aquitaine, with a brilliant and extravagant court at Bordeaux, led an expedition into Spain to restore Pedro the Cruel to the throne of Castile, an adventure from which he returned with a disease that was to kill him nine years later. In 1368 his brother Lionel, now Duke of Clarence, married as his second wife Violante Visconti, daughter of the immensely wealthy Lord of Pavia, and died in Italy, possibly by poison. Then, the summer of 1369 was disastrously wet, and severe plague returned to England. In August Queen Philippa died, holding her husband's hand and imploring him that, when his time came, he would lie beside her 'in the cloister at Westminster'. Among the mourners were Geoffrey and Philippa Chaucer, dressed in black provided by the King's Wardrobe. A

'O noble, O worthy Petro, glory of Spaine,
Whom Fortune held so high in majestee,
Well oughten men thy piteous death complaine!'

'. . . the resemblaunce
Of him that hath in me so fresh lyflinesse
That to putte othere men in remembraunce
Of his persone I have heer his lyknesse
Do make.'

Hoccleve has Chaucer's portrait painted beside the verse which pays tribute to his 'master dear'. ▶

tifie

resemblaunce

nesse

enbraunce

knesse

iesse

ght & mynde

a fynde

a

so seyntes

& seen

restreyntes

axeynt is

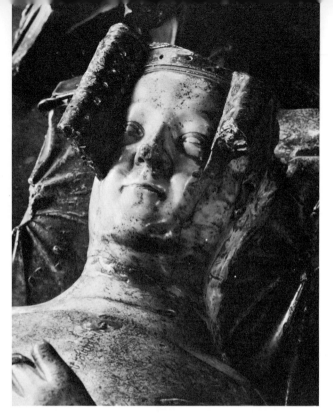

Philippa of Hainault, 'the good Queen of England, who had done so many praiseworthy actions in the course of her life.' Froissart.

'... Farewell, sweet,
And farewell all that ever there is.'
The tomb of Blanche, Duchess of Lancaster, beside whom John of Gaunt was later buried. ▶

few weeks later, John of Gaunt's wife, Blanche of Lancaster, died, aged only twenty-seven.

While Blanche lay dying, her husband was ravaging France between Calais and Boulogne, and the Black Prince, too ill to ride a horse, prepared to besiege Limoges, which was sacked and gutted after the slaughter of all its inhabitants. Edward III had reasserted his claim to the French throne, and renewed the Hundred Years War. He was, however, sinking into premature senility in the arms, or in the clutches, of his mistress Alice Perrers, an audacious, avaricious woman to whom he could refuse nothing.

In that miserable summer of 1369 Chaucer was paid £10 as 'equitanti de guerre in partibus Francie', a mounted soldier, probably on John of Gaunt's expedition into northern France, where he would learn something more about fourteenth-century chivalry:

> The shippen brenning in the blacke smoke . . .
> The open war, with woundes all bi-bledde.

The death of the Queen meant that Philippa Chaucer lost her post at Court, and it would naturally be to his old acquaintance, possibly boyhood friend, John of Gaunt, that Chaucer turned for patronage. As the Duchess Blanche died soon after the Queen, however, there was no post for his wife in the Duke's household, but Chaucer wrote an elegy for him, *The Book of the Duchess*.

Although his first original long poem, it is written in the conventional manner of the fashionable French school, much of the matter being taken from Guillaume de Machault and Ovid: another tale of courtly love in a medieval dream world. Yet there are passages of realistic description and dialogue that prefigure the poet of *The Canterbury Tales*.

*The Book of the Duchess*

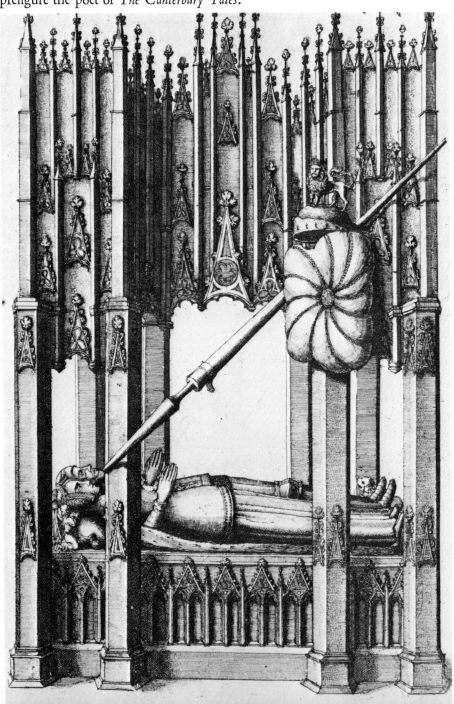

'I holde hit be a sicknesse
That I have suffred this
            eight yeare,
The lovesick and sleepless
poet.'

'Ah! mercy! sweete lady
deare!
Help me out of this
distresse.'

A page from Machaut's *Dit de la Fontaine Amoureuse*, to which Chaucer was indebted.

Chaucer imagines himself lovelorn and sleepless, and tells how, after reading Ovid's story of Ceyx and Alcyone, he promises Morpheus 'the best gift he ever had in his life', a feather-bed with linen sheets and pillowcases, if only he will send him the gift of sleep. He falls asleep, and dreams that he wakes on a May morning – the conventional month of love – to the singing of birds on the roof. The sun is shining through the stained-glass windows that illustrate *The Romance of the Rose*, when he hears the sound of a horn, dresses quickly, mounts his horse and joins the hunt. The hart escapes, and as he is walking alone,

> there came by me
> A whelp that fawned me as I stood,
> That had y-followed, and coude no good.
> It come and crept to me as lowe
> Right as it hadde me y-knowe,
> Held down his head and joined his eares,
> And laid all smoothe down his haires.

38

He follows the puppy through a wood until he sees a man in black sitting against an oak tree, a handsome young knight of twenty-four. It is John of Gaunt, though both he and Chaucer were twenty-nine when the Duchess died. The sorrowful knight complains to himself:

*'I have of sorrow so great woon*
*That joye get I never none,*
*Now that I see my lady bright,*
*Which I have loved with all my might,*
*Is fro me dead and is a-gone.'*

Richmond Castle, Yorkshire.
'A long castel with walles white
By Seynt Johan! on a rich hill.'
Chaucer's tribute to John of Gaunt, Earl of Richmond, and his dead wife Blanche (white).

At length he notices Chaucer, who, after an exchange of courtesies, tells him that the hunt is over, the hart escaped. The knight is not interested, 'For I am sorrow, and sorrow is I.' Encouraged by Chaucer to talk, he describes his loss in terms of a game of chess with 'false Fortune', who has taken his queen and checkmated him with a pawn. Now, he only longs for death.

One of Chaucer's most endearing qualities is his way of making fun of himself, and he now adds a characteristically humorous episode. He understands John of Gaunt literally, tells him that even if he had lost all his chessmen he has no right to think of suicide: 'Remember Socrates!' and he quotes a number of classical examples.

The knight tells Chaucer that he does not understand him, and patiently describes how he fell in love with 'White':

> *I saw hir daunce so comlily,*
> *Carol and sing so sweetely,*
> *Laugh and pley so womanly,*
> *And looke so debónairly,*
> *So goodly speak and so frendly.*

Then, according to Cicero's rules of rhetoric, as codified by Matthew de Vendôme and Chaucer's 'dear master' Geoffrey de Vinsauf, the knight describes his lady – though like Chaucer himself he professes to lack both

'At chess with me she gan to play.'

'And all men speaken of hunting,
How they would slay the hart
with strength.'

Savoy

(*left*) John of Gaunt quarters the
arms of his second wife, Constance,
on his shield: the castle and lion of
Castile and Leon.

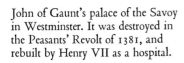

John of Gaunt:
'A wonder well-faring knight.'

John of Gaunt's palace of the Savoy
in Westminster. It was destroyed in
the Peasants' Revolt of 1381, and
rebuilt by Henry VII as a hospital.

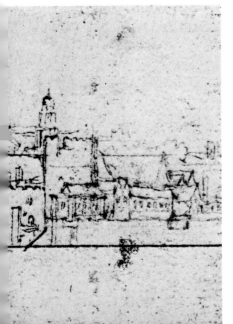

43

English and wit to do so – working down from her golden hair to her eyes, face, neck, shoulders, arms, hands, nails, breasts, hips and 'straight flat back'. She was as good as she was beautiful, as good as her loss is insupportable.

> *'What loss is that, sir?' quod I tho;*
> *'Will she not love you? is it so?*
> *Or have ye oughte done amiss,*
> *That she hath left you? is it this?'*

The knight continues his explanation to the impenetrable poet: how at last he plucked up courage to tell White of his love, and was repulsed, but how, after the conventional year of service, she gave him 'the noble gift of her mercy', and for many a year they lived happily together.

Until this point the pace has been a leisurely, digressive, medieval one, but now there is a sudden tension, and Chaucer finishes the story with a burst of dramatic dialogue:

> *'Sir,' quod I, 'where is she now?'*
> *'Now?' quod he, and stint anone.*
> *Therewith he wax as dead as stone,*
> *And said, 'Alas, that I was bore!*
> *That was the loss that here-before*
> *I tolde thee that I had lorn . . .*
> *God wot, alas! right that was she!'*
> *'Alas, sir, how? what may that be?'*
> *'She is dead!' 'Nay!' 'Yis, by my truthe!'*
> *'Is that your loss? By God, 'tis ruthe!'*
> *And with that worde, right anone,*
> *They gan to strake forth; all was done,*
> *For that time, the hart-hunting.*

The hart-hunting was done! And never before in English literature had there been anything like these last few lines of *The Book of the Duchess*.

John of Gaunt buried his Duchess in St Paul's Cathedral, handsomely in alabaster, the new material for princes' tombs. He was immensely wealthy, the Duke of Lancaster, holding all the vast Lancastrian possessions in his own right, and in 1372 he tried still further to exalt his state by marrying Constance, elder daughter of Pedro the Cruel, King of Castile. Although Pedro had been murdered by his bastard brother, who seized the throne, John of Gaunt was not deterred from claiming the throne himself and adding the title of King of Castile to that of Duke of Lancaster. This second marriage was merely one of convenience, for his real love was the newly widowed Katherine Swynford,

French Flamboyant: rose window, Évreux Cathedral.

English Perpendicular: great east window,
Gloucester Cathedral.

who now became his mistress, living in his palace of the Savoy near West-minster, nominally as his children's governess. It is not surprising, therefore, that Katherine's sister, Philippa Chaucer, should be taken into the Duke's household as lady-in-waiting to his new Duchess, and in August 1372 he granted her a pension of £10 a year in consideration of her past and future services to his dear wife, 'the Queen of Castile'. A few months later he added a button-hook and six silver-gilt buttons as a New Year's gift.

*The first*
*English poets* Chaucer himself, part courtier, responsible for entertaining the Court with his poetry, part civil servant, was now employed in a series of diplomatic missions for the King, the first of which was in the summer of 1370. His journey was not a long one, for he was back in London by October, when he was paid his half-yearly salary. It may have been at about this time that he wrote *An A.B.C.* and *The Complaint unto Pity*, the first a poem of about two hundred lines, the other half its length. *An A.B.C.* is a very free translation of a prayer to the Virgin by a French monk, each successive stanza beginning with the corresponding letter of the alphabet. As poetry there is nothing very remarkable about it, but as verse it is important. The French original is in octosyllabics, like most French, and therefore English, verse of the period, but Chaucer's adaptation is in a line of ten syllables, the line that he was to establish as the staple one of English poetry. *The Complaint unto Pity* is a lover's complaint in the conventional French manner, but again important for its metrical form, the seven-line stanza, or rhyme royal, apparently its first use in English:

> *Pity, that I have sought so yore ago,*
> *With hearte sore, and full of busy paine,*
> *That in this world was never wight so woe*
> *Withoute death; and if I shall not feigne,*
> *My purpose was to Pity to complaine*
> *Upon the cruelty and tyrannye*
> *Of love, that for my truthe doth me die.*

Rhyme royal became Chaucer's favourite stanza, and the medium of a number of his tales, notably *Troilus and Criseyde*.

The war with France had provoked a new spirit of nationalism and an anti-French feeling in England. In 1362 English replaced French as the language of the law courts, and during the next twenty years 'in alle the gramere scoles of Engelond, children leveth Frensche and construeth and lerneth in Englische,' so that they 'conneth no more Frensche than can their left heele.' Even archi-tecture in the two countries diverged: French Gothic becoming increasingly curvilinear, or Flamboyant, English rectilinear, or Perpendicular. Perhaps the alliterative revival in English poetry was another symptom of nationalism. This

Piers Plowman falls asleep.    Pearl and her father.    The Green Knight.

was an attempt to revive the Old English, loosely rhythmical line of four
stresses, in which the convention is alliteration, the repetition of an initial letter
or sound, instead of a regular metre and rhyme. The most famous of these
poems is *The Vision of Piers the Plowman*, written in the West Midland dialect
by William Langland, his first version dating from the 1360s:

> *In a summer season when softe was the sunne,*
> *I schop me into a schroud a scheep as I were;*
> *In habit of an hermit unholy of workes,*
> *Went I wide in this world wondres to heare.*
> *But in a Mays morning on Malvern hilles*
> *Me befell a ferly. . . . .*

It is a dream poem in the medieval manner, not of courtly love, however, but a
series of vivid visions revealing the abuses and mounting social unrest of the age.

Then, while Chaucer was writing *The Book of the Duchess* in the East
Midland dialect of London, an unknown poet was writing another elegy in the
North Western dialect. This was *Pearl*, the dream of a father who sees his dead
daughter Pearl on the other side of a river, which he longs to cross. It is a very
beautiful and accomplished poem, for in an elaborate stanza the poet combines
the new convention of regular metre and rhyme with the old convention of
alliteration:

47

'Moral Gower': his head resting on his principal works. The effigy in the church of St Mary Overy, now Southwark Cathedral.

> *From spot my spirit there sprang in space,*
> *My body on balke there bode in sweven,*
> *My ghost is gone in Godes grace*
> *In aventure where marvels meven.*

The poet of *Pearl* was probably the author of *Sir Gawain and the Green Knight*, an enchanting romance in alliterative verse interspersed with rhyming quatrains.

Chaucer's friend John Gower was, in a way, even more old-fashioned; he had not yet got as far as writing in English, and at this time was probably finishing his *Mirour de l'Omme*, a moralizing poem of fifteen thousand French octosyllabic couplets. His next work was to be *Vox Clamantis*, another poem of epic proportions, this time in Latin.

Chaucer, however, was not only writing in English, but also experimenting in new metrical forms, and as English was becoming the language of the educated classes, the number of his readers increased. The future lay with him, though in 1372 he was still under the influence of French culture and courtly conventions. We can imagine him at this time: a young man of thirty-two, brought up in princely and royal households, well-mannered, courteous, accomplished, with some experience of military service and a knowledge of northern France. However, he was of middle-class origin, and acquainted therefore with all ranks of society, interested in everything, with a hawk's eye for significant detail, and an impish sense of humour and the ridiculous; an omnivorous reader, probably not a great talker, but a most attentive listener, modest, tolerant, but critical: a sensitive, impressionable, questing young man, whom any new stimulus might jolt out of the old French convention of courtly make-believe as the proper subject-matter of poetry.

48

Such a stimulus came in November 1372, when the King sent his 'scutifer', his esquire Geoffrey Chaucer, on a diplomatic mission to Italy, with two Genoese as his companions. Their objective was Genoa, where they were to treat with the Duke about a suitable English port for Genoese trade. Chaucer received an advance of £66 for his expenses, and probably reached Genoa early in 1373. Even in winter the journey through France would be an exhilaration, but Italy in spring a revelation. Even more important than Genoa was his visit to Florence, to which he was sent on secret business, possibly to negotiate a loan. Florence was a great financial and industrial centre, but it was also the city in which the seeds of the Renaissance were stirring: the city of Giotto, with whom modern painting may be said to have begun, and Chaucer would see the campanile that he had designed for the cathedral nearing completion. Giotto's friend Dante had been born in Florence, though he had died in exile fifty years before Chaucer's visit. He does not seem to have heard of Boccaccio at this time, and never mentions him in his work, though it is just possible that he met Boccaccio's dearest friend, Petrarch, making the 150-mile journey to

Dante, 'the grete poet of Itaille', and
Petrarch, 'the laureat poete'.

Medieval Genoa.

The countryside of Tuscany that Chaucer passed through.

Genoese money-lenders.

Fourteenth-century Florence.

'The Queen herself sitting as a Justise.'
Giotto's personification of Justice.

Scenes from Boccaccio's *Decameron*. Panel from an Italian marriage-chest, *c.* 1420.

Dartmouth, visited by Chaucer in 1373. ▶

Padua to greet the great Italian poet and humanist who had begun the revival of learning in medieval Europe. It is possible, for in *The Canterbury Tales* Chaucer was to make his Clerk of Oxford say:

> *I will you tell a tale which that I*
> *Learned at Padowe of a worthy clerk,*
> *As proved by his wordes and his werk.*
> *He is now dead and nailed in his cheste,*
> *I pray to God to give his soule reste!*
> *Fraunceys Petrark, the laureat poete,*
> *Highte this clerk, whose rhetoryke sweete*
> *Enlumined all Itaille of poetry.*

It seems improbable that this poor Oxford scholar could ever have met Petrarch in Padua, and it may be that Chaucer himself is speaking through the mouth of one of his characters. The Clerk's tale of patient Griselda is the last in Boccaccio's *Decameron*, but Chaucer's source was Petrarch's Latin adaptation of the story. He must have brought a number of manuscripts back to England, and after his return spent much of his time reading the Italian literature of his age: finding new inspiration in the poetry of Petrarch and vivid realistic descriptions of Dante, which were so much to influence his own work.

52

Evidently his mission had been a success, for soon after his return in the early summer of 1373 he was sent to Dartmouth to investigate the claim of a Genoese sea-captain, that after his ship had been wrecked off the Devonshire coast, it had been looted by the natives. He may have been right, and it is significant that Chaucer tells us that the piratical shipman among his Canterbury pilgrims probably came from Dartmouth.

In February 1374 he received the balance of his expenses for his Italian mission, and on 23 April, at the annual celebration of the Festival of St George at Windsor, the King awarded his 'beloved esquire', his 'dilecto Armigero Galfrido Chaucer', a daily pitcher of wine. A few weeks later he received his first government appointment: as Controller of the Customs and Subsidy of

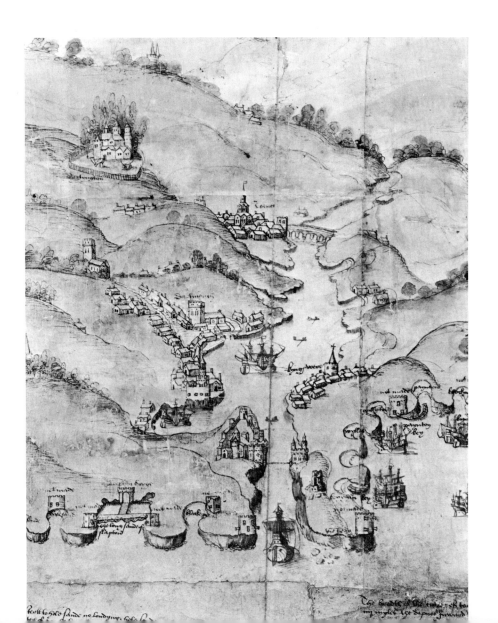

Geoffrey Chaucer's seal, used by Thomas Chaucer in 1409.

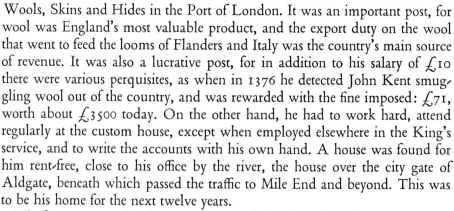

Wools, Skins and Hides in the Port of London. It was an important post, for wool was England's most valuable product, and the export duty on the wool that went to feed the looms of Flanders and Italy was the country's main source of revenue. It was also a lucrative post, for in addition to his salary of £10 there were various perquisites, as when in 1376 he detected John Kent smuggling wool out of the country, and was rewarded with the fine imposed: £71, worth about £3500 today. On the other hand, he had to work hard, attend regularly at the custom house, except when employed elsewhere in the King's service, and to write the accounts with his own hand. A house was found for him rent-free, close to his office by the river, the house over the city gate of Aldgate, beneath which passed the traffic to Mile End and beyond. This was to be his home for the next twelve years.

His fortunes were in the ascendant, and the day after taking his oath as Controller, John of Gaunt granted him a pension of £10 for life, in return for his and his wife's services to his mother, the late Queen Philippa, and to his wife the Queen of Castile. Then, in the following year he was given the wardship of two boys, whose estates he was to manage until they came of age: valuable offices, one of which brought in £104 during the next three years.

His work as Controller left him little time for reading and writing, yet he did find time, as he tells us himself in a humorous description of his life at Aldgate:

English seal of the delivery of wools and hides, and seal of the Port of London.

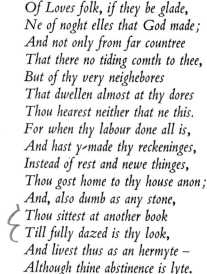

> thou hast no tidinges
> Of Loves folk, if they be glade,
> Ne of noght elles that God made;
> And not only from far countree
> That there no tiding comth to thee,
> But of thy very neighebores
> That dwellen almost at thy dores
> Thou hearest neither that ne this.
> For when thy labour done all is,
> And hast y-made thy reckeninges,
> Instead of rest and newe thinges,
> Thou gost home to thy house anon;
> And, also dumb as any stone,
> Thou sittest at another book
> Till fully dazed is thy look,
> And livest thus as an hermyte –
> Although thine abstinence is lyte.

He practised little abstinence. Although an enforced recluse at this time, Chaucer was no ascetic, but loved the good things of this delightful world.

54

The passage comes from *The House of Fame*, an unfinished poem that bears witness to his recent reading of Dante, and Dante's guide Virgil, as well as of his old favourites, Ovid in particular, a copy of whose *Metamorphoses* he tells us he possessed. But, although these writers supplied him with hints, and sometimes whole episodes, the story and its treatment are essentially original. It is written in conventional octosyllabics, and begins in the usual medieval manner with a dream. Dreams and their meaning always fascinated Chaucer, and were for him philosophically important; for if they foretold the future, there was at least an element of predestination in man's life, a limit to his freedom of choice.

'A feminine creature . . .
That with her feet she earthe reighte,
And with her head she touched heavene,
There as shinen starres sevene.'

On the night of 10 December he falls asleep, and dreams that he is inside the Temple of Venus, which is adorned with 'images' and a brass tablet inscribed with the opening lines of the *Aeneid*:

> *I will now sing, if that I can,*
> *The armes, and also the man. . .*

which serves as a pretext for a summary of Virgil's epic.

Book I is undistinguished, but in Book II Chaucer gives rein to his imagination and humour. It begins with an appeal to 'every manner man that English understande can' to listen to his further adventures. As he is roaming in a field, a soaring eagle sees him,

> *And with his grimme pawes stronge,*
> *Within his sharpe nailes longe,*
> *Me, fleeing, at a swoop he hente,*
> *And with a spring again up wente,*
> *Me carrying in his clawes starke*
> *As lightly as I were a larke.*

He is so terrified that he faints, until the eagle calls, 'Awak! for shame!'

> *'Awak!' to me he said,*
> *Right in the same voice and tone*
> *That useth one I coulde name;*
> *And with that voice, sooth for to sayn,*
> *My minde came to me again;*
> *For it was goodly said to me,*
> *As was it never wont to be.*

Either Philippa Chaucer had a sharp tongue that recalled Chaucer from his imaginative flights back to the solid Aldgate house, or, much more probably, it is an affectionate joke, the kind of joke that would raise a laugh when he read the poem aloud at Court, with Philippa in the audience.

The eagle is a kindly and most informative bird who, though he has a low opinion of Chaucer's intelligence – 'In thy head full little is' – gives a detailed and remarkably scientific explanation of sound-waves. They are now in the region of 'eyrish bestes', of the animal Signs of the Zodiac, and of the Milky Way, as full of stars as Watling Street, by St Paul's, is full of people. 'Wilt thou learn of starres ought?' the eagle asks hopefully; but 'No,' Chaucer replies firmly, 'certainly not. I am too old.' A strange reply from one so well read in astronomy, and eager to learn more.

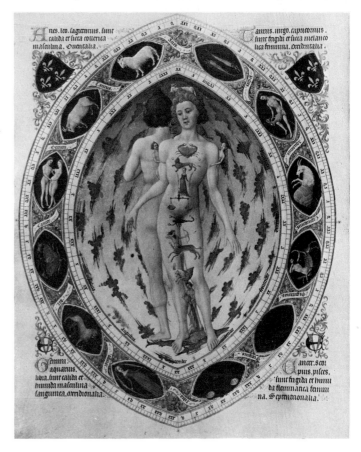

A Zodiac Man. 'And everich of these twelve signs hath respect to a certain parcel of the body of a man, and hath it in governance; as Aries hath thine head, and Taurus thy neck and thy throat, Gemini thine arms, and so forth.' *The Astrolabe.*

At last they sight the House of Fame, and in Book III the eagle leaves Chaucer to explore. It is a palace on a melting glacier, crowded with people who are the embodiments of the words they speak on earth. Here is Fame enthroned, 'a feminine creature' who quite arbitrarily dispenses renown, slander, infamy or oblivion to deservers and undeservers alike. A man taps Chaucer on the shoulder, and asks him if he has come to find fame.

> *'Nay, forsoothe, friend!' quod I;*
> *'I came not hither, grant mercy,*
> *For no such cause, by my head!*
> *Sufficeth me, as I were dead,*
> *That no wight have my name in hande.*
> *I wot myself best how I stande;*
> *For what I dure or what I thinke,*
> *I will myselven all it drinke,*
> *Certain, for the more part,*
> *As farforth as I can mine art.'*

57

He has come to find tidings of love, he adds. The man then takes him to the House of Rumour, a huge, whirling, wickerwork structure, where pilgrims, shipmen, pardoners and other travellers, with bags and boxes full of lies, whisper sibilant false tidings:

*'Knowst not thou*
*What is betid, lo, late or now?'*
*'No,' quod he, 'telle me what.'*
*And then he told him this and that,*
*And swore thereto that it was sooth –*
*'Thus hath he said' – and 'Thus he dooth' –*
*'Thus shall it be' – 'Thus heard I say' –*
*'That shall be found' – 'That dare I lay.'*

At last Chaucer sees someone who appears to be 'a man of great authority', but who he was we do not know, for with these words the poem abruptly ends. It is a pity; we would give much to have further self-revelations, for in this delightful fantasy we catch a glimpse of Chaucer as he was being transformed from a writer of conventional love-poetry into a master of the new realism.

Other poems of these last years of Edward III were probably *The Complaint of Mars* and *A Complaint to his Lady*, interesting mainly as experiments in rhyme royal, in a nine-line stanza, and in the *terza rima* of Dante, its first employment in English:

> *Her love I best, and shall, while I may dure,*
> *Bet than myself an hundred thousand deal,*
> *Than all this world's richesse of creature.*
> *Now hath not Love me bestowed weel*
> *To love there I never shall have part?*
> *Alas! right thus is turned me the wheel,*
> *Thus am I slain with Loves fiery dart. . . .*

Then there was *The Life of St Cecilia*, which was to be inserted in *The Canter-bury Tales* as the Second Nun's contribution. It is little more than a translation of a Latin original, but admirably told in rhyme royal. Chaucer was a devoted son of the Catholic Church, but he must have smiled as he described the martyrdom of the virtuous lady, condemned to burn 'in a bath of flames red':

> *The longe night, and eek a day also,*
> *For all the fire and eek the bathes heate,*
> *She sat all cold, and feelede no woe:*
> *It made her not a drope for to sweate.*

The last years of Edward III's reign were a period of disenchantment and profound discontent. Agricultural labourers were angered by the attempt of landowners to keep down wages and force them back into serfdom, and echoed the words of the itinerant communist priest John Ball, who asked:  *Troubled times*

> *When Adam delved and Eve span,*
> *Who was then the gentleman?*

(*left*) Bodiam Castle, Sussex, a symmetrical and moated fortress built in the 1380s as a defence against threatened French invasion.

'Three strokes in the neck he smote her then.'
The martyrdom of St Cecilia.

Adam digs, and Eve spins.

Workers in the towns resented the widening gap between themselves and their masters; weavers in the new English cloth industry resented the competition of Flemish immigrants, and London financiers the establishment of Lombard bankers in their city. Taxation was heavy to pay for the French war, which was now little more than a series of disasters, and as the chief ministers were mainly clergy, much of the discontent was directed against the Church. There was little respect in England for the Papacy, for during the greater part of the fourteenth century the Popes were mostly Frenchmen, living in dissolute splendour in 'the sinful city of Avignon'. Corruption spread through all branches of the Church, and it was against its wealth and worldliness and interference in the government of the country that John Wycliffe was so passionately preaching.

Flemish weavers' cottages, Lavenham, Suffolk.

◀ The Papal Palace, Avignon.

Fourteenth-century tithe-barn, Bradford-on-Avon. The payment of tithes, a tenth part of their produce, was one of the peasants' grievances.

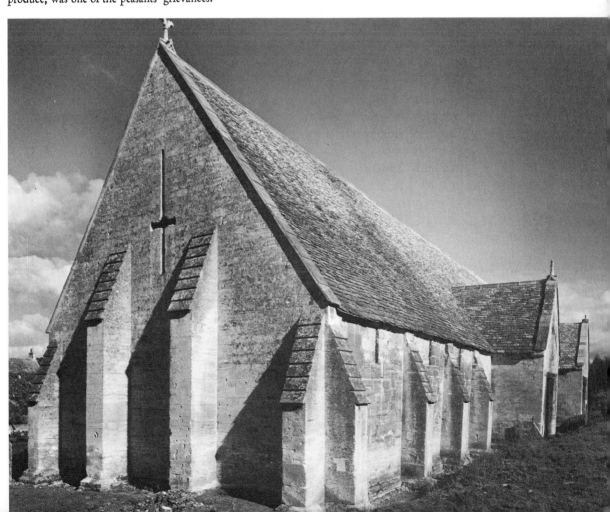

The Black Prince (1330–76),
eldest son of Edward III, and father of Richard II.

The King was in his dotage, a prematurely aged man, and now a struggle among his sons began for control of the government. John of Gaunt sought popularity by supporting Wycliffe and the anti-clerical party, which was backed by the King's mistress, Alice Perrers, and the London financiers. In 1371 he managed to get rid of the Chancellor, William of Wykeham, Bishop of Winchester, but the new government was as unsuccessful as the old, and the London citizens were incensed by the corruption and maladministration of this Court party. When the Black Prince returned from Aquitaine, a dying man, he formed an opposition party which, in the Parliament of 1376, attacked the government, imprisoned two of its leaders, and banished Alice Perrers from the Court. In June, however, the Black Prince died, and the work of the 'Good Parliament' was undone by its successor. John of Gaunt packed this Parliament with his own supporters, the imprisoned ministers were released, and Alice Perrers was recalled to Court. He overstepped himself, however, by trying to take the government of London out of the hands of the Mayor and put it under the King's control, and when on 19 February 1377 he appeared in St Paul's Cathedral in defence of Wycliffe, who was charged with heresy, he had to fly for his life from the infuriated citizens.

62

William of Wykeham (1324-1404), Bishop of Winchester, Chancellor of England, and founder of Winchester College and New College, Oxford.

Chaucer was abroad at this time, and must have heard of these events with misgiving, for his wife was still employed by John of Gaunt, and the Duke's pensions of £10 each were a substantial part of their income. In December 1376 he had been sent to France on secret negotiations, presumably for peace, in association with Sir John Burley, Captain of Calais. Then, on 17 February 1377, two days before the affair in St Paul's, he set off for Paris and Montreuil with Sir Thomas Percy, to help to negotiate the marriage of Richard, the ten-year-old son of the Black Prince, and Marie, the seven-year-old daughter of Charles V of France. He was back in London by the end of March, when he would report to the King, or more probably to Alice Perrers or John of Gaunt, after which he returned to France. Princess Marie died in May, however, negotiations broke down, and some of the delegates sailed for England, only to be killed by French pirates in the Channel. Chaucer was more fortunate, but when he reached England on 26 June he learned that the King had just died. Deserted by his courtiers, and robbed by Alice Perrers of all that she could carry, even the rings on his fingers, he was left with a solitary priest to close his eyes. Of his former vast possessions in France, only the ports of Calais, Cherbourg, Brest, Bordeaux and Bayonne remained in English hands.

63

PARIS

Chaucer went on
a diplomatic mission
to Paris in 1377.

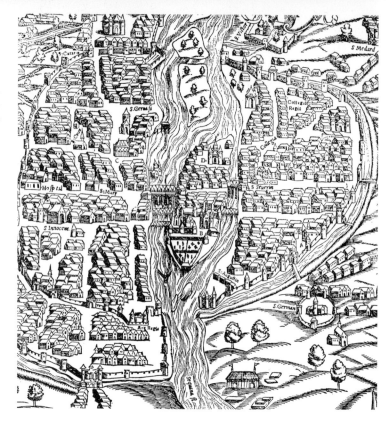

The walled city.
Notre Dame on the
Ile de la Cité.

Edward III (1312–77), whom Chaucer had served for some fifteen years.

The accession of the boy-king Richard II made no difference in Chaucer's position. He was confirmed in his office of Controller of the Customs, received his usual salary of twenty marks as one of the King's esquires, with an additional £2 for robes, and another twenty marks a year in lieu of his daily pitcher of wine. He was a wealthy man, with a tax-free income that was the equivalent of about £4000 today. As further proof of the confidence which was placed in him, he was sent to France in January 1378 as a member of a deputation to renew negotiations for peace. They failed, and the government decided to send another expedition into France. John of Gaunt was paid £4000 for his army, and on

The boy king Richard II holding court.

the same day Chaucer received £66 towards the expenses of a journey to Milan, where he and his companion Sir Edward Berkeley were to discuss 'certain matters concerning the King's expedition of war'. He had been abroad so much in the previous year that he had been allowed to appoint a temporary deputy at the Wool Customs, and now, having given powers of attorney to his friend John Gower, he set off with his companion; Berkeley with ten attendants, himself with six.

In Milan they were to treat with its ruler, Bernabo Visconti, and Sir John Hawkwood, the famous English mercenary soldier, who had recently married one of Bernabo's numerous illegitimate daughters. No doubt the negotiations were to raise a loan from the wealthy Visconti, and to enlist the support of Hawkwood and his White Company, though what the outcome was remains unknown. More important was the impact on Chaucer of this second visit to Italy, of its countryside and walled city of Milan, its churches, palaces and pictures. Then, ruthless tyrant though he was, Bernabo Visconti was a generous patron of the arts and collector of books, and may have helped Chaucer to find the sort of manuscript he was looking for: contemporary Italian verse and prose. Evidently Bernabo impressed him, for when he came to write the *Monk's Tale* a few years later, he cited him as a tragic victim of false Fortune, one of those who fell from high estate into adversity.

Chaucer was back in London by the middle of September, probably bringing with him manuscript copies of Boccaccio's epic, *Il Teseide*, the story of King Theseus and two knights, and his romance, *Il Filostrato*, two poems that were to have an immense influence on his later work.

'Of Milan greate Barnabo Viscounte,
God of delight, and scourge of Lombardye,
Why should I not thine infortune recounte,
Sith in estaat thou clombe were so hye?
Thy brother son, that was thy double allye,
For he thy nevew was, and son-in-lawe,
Within his prison made thee to die;
But why, ne how, noot I that thou were slawe.'

It was probably soon after his return from Italy that he wrote, or rather began, *Anelida and Arcite*. The poem opens in epic style with an invocation to Mars and the Muses to help him in his song: three stanzas taken from the *Teseide*. There follows the story of how the young Queen Anelida pines for love of the faithless Arcite, until in desperation she appeals to him in a *Complaint*. Chaucer was essentially a narrative and dramatic poet, but in the complex stanzas of Anelida's *Complaint* he shows his powers as a lyric poet as well:

> *For thogh I hadde you tomorrow again,*
> *I might as well hold Aperil from rain,*
> *As holde you, to make you stedfast.*
> *Almighty God, of truthe sovereyn,*
> *Where is the truth of man? Who hath it slain?*
> *Who that them loveth shall them find as fast*
> *As in a tempest is a rotten mast.*
> *Is that a tame beast that is ay fain*
> *To run away, when he is least aghast?*

After this lyrical digression, Chaucer resumes his story, telling how Anelida vows to sacrifice to Mars in his temple, 'That shapen was as ye shall after hear.' But at this line Chaucer stopped. Perhaps he found that the Italian epic style and conventional French theme of courtly love could not be reconciled satisfactorily, or perhaps he was interrupted by the strange case of Cecily Chaumpaigne, who in May 1380 released him from all her rights of action 'tam de raptu meo'.

Sir John Hawkwood (d. 1394), the English mercenary soldier, who, with his White Company, won great wealth and renown in the Italian wars of Chaucer's time.

67

It is most unlikely that Chaucer, a distinguished man of forty, was guilty of assaulting a woman, and the word 'rape' most probably refers to an abduction similar to that of Chaucer's father, who, as a boy, was carried off in an attempt to marry him to his cousin. It does not follow that Chaucer was deeply involved in the affair, but, whatever the reason, he did not continue *Anelida and Arcite*, and the description of the Temple of Mars had to wait until he wrote the story of another, true Arcite in *The Knight's Tale*.

Instead, he turned again to the medieval dream-world, though with the *Teseide* still in mind, and began *The Parliament of Fowls*, a poem inspired, partly at least, by his love of birds:

> *The life so short, the craft so long to learne,*
> *Th'assay so hard, so sharp the conqueringe,*
> *The dreadful joy that alway slip so yerne. . . .*

The splendid opening might well refer to the art of poetry and his own struggle for perfection, but it is of the art of love that he is writing, an art of which he professes ignorance in practice, for all his knowledge comes from books, the reading of which is his chief delight.

While he was reading Cicero's *Dream of Scipio*,

> *The day gan failen, and the darke night,*
> *That reaveth beastes from their businesse,*
> *Berefte me my book for lack of light.*

The lines are Dante's, and when he falls asleep Scipio Africanus appears to him in a dream, and, as Virgil led Dante, so Scipio leads Chaucer to the gates, not of Hell, but of the Garden of Love. He hesitates to enter, for though on one gate is written, 'Through me men go into that blissful place,' on the other he sees, 'Through me men go unto the mortal strokes of the spear.' Scipio, however, 'shoof' him inside, telling him that he has nothing to fear, 'For thou of love hast lost thy taste,'

> *'But natheless, although that thou be dull,*
> *Yet that thou canst not do, yet mayst thou see;*
> *For many a man that may not stand a pull,*
> *It liketh him at the wrestling for to be.'*

There follow a hundred lines from the *Teseide*, describing the garden in the more sensuous Italian manner, until at length, 'In a glade, upon a hill of flowers', Chaucer sees the goddess Nature surrounded by birds of all kinds; for it is St Valentine's Day, when every bird comes there to choose its mate. The catalogue of birds, from 'royal eagle' to 'waker goose' and 'frosty fieldfare' is a masterpiece of concise and vivid description.

68

Now begins the Chaucerian fun. First, a mate is to be chosen for a gentle female eagle who has three suitors, all of whom swear to serve her according to the code of courtly love. The courteous pleading goes on so long that the common birds grow restive, as they cannot mate until the dispute of the royal eagles is settled.

> *'Come off!' they cried, 'Alas, ye will us shende!*
> *When shall your cursed pleading have an end?'* . . .
> *The goose, the cuckoo and the duck also*
> *So criede 'kek-kek! kuckoo! queck-queck!' high.*
> *That through mine ears the noise wente tho.*

To quieten them and make an end, Nature decrees that one bird of every kind shall speak for the rest, and say which of the three suitors is worthiest. The falcon speaks for the nobility, the predatory birds of the House of Lords, and stuffily suggests that they should fight it out: 'There must be batayle.' Then come the verdicts of the Commons. The goose, speaking for the water-fowl, loses no time: 'My mind is sharp,' she says, 'if she won't love him, let him love another.' The sentimental turtle-dove, representing the seed-fowl, protests: 'Let him serve her ever, till he be dead.' The duck laughs vulgarly at this: 'By my hat! That men should alway loven, causeless!' Then impatiently the cuckoo, speaking for the worm-fowl, cries: 'Let each of them be single all his life.'

> 'The sparrow, Venus son; the nightingale,
> That clepeth forth the freshe leaves newe;
> The swallow, murdrer of the flyes smalle,
> That maken honey of flowres fresh of hue;
> The wedded turtle, with her hearte true;
> The peacock, with his aungels feathers brighte;
> The pheasant, scorner of the cock by night.'

69

Nature quells the ensuing uproar, and finally gives her decision: the suitors shall serve the lady for a year, when she herself shall choose the one she loves best. Nature now gives all the other birds their mates, and they depart lovingly, all but a choir of song-birds, who sing a roundel in honour of the goddess, the only roundel remaining of the many that Chaucer is said to have written:

> *Now welcome, summer, with thy sunne softe,*
> *That hast this winter weather overshake,*
> *And driven away the longe nightes blake!*
>
> *Saint Valentine, that art full high on-lofte,*
> *Thus singen smalle fowles for thy sake:*
> *Now welcome, summer, with thy sunne softe,*
> *That hast this winter weather overtake.*
>
> *Well have they cause for to gladen ofte,*
> *Sith each of them recovered hath his make;*
> *Full blissful may they singen when they wake:*
> *Now welcome, summer, with thy sunne softe,*
> *That hast this winter weather overtake,*
> *And driven away the longe nightes blake.*

With the shouting when the song is done, Chaucer wakes, reaches for another book, and begins to read.

*The Parliament of Fowls* may be an allegory: the first suitor being Richard II, and the gentle female eagle Princess Marie of France, or Philippa of Lancaster, daughter of John of Gaunt, who wished to marry her to his nephew, or Princess Anne of Bohemia, whom Richard did marry early in 1382. But the poem may be simply a burlesque of courtly love, the artificiality of which by now appeared to Chaucer, far more interested in real life than in make-believe, as slightly ludicrous. In any event, it is one of his most delightful poems, one of the most delightful in the language.

It was probably written shortly before the Peasants' Revolt, when the discontent that had been smouldering for most of Chaucer's lifetime suddenly erupted in June 1381. The underlying causes were serfdom and low wages, but the immediate cause was a poll-tax that fell more heavily on the poor than on the rich. There were risings throughout the country, where manors were sacked and records burned, but the main events took place in London and its neighbourhood. Led by Wat Tyler, the peasants converged on the capital, whose citizens rose in their support. The fourteen-year-old King managed to appease the Essex men at Mile End by promising the abolition of serfdom, but meanwhile the men of Kent forced London Bridge and seized the Tower, murdered

The Peasants' Revolt, 1381. Wat Tyler threatens the Mayor of London, who is about to draw his sword and strike him.

The Tower of London and London Bridge. The Custom House where Chaucer worked lay between the two.

Labourers' passes. After the Peasants' Revolt the movement of workers was restricted by statute.

the gentle Archbishop Sudbury, unpopular ministers and Flemish weavers, and burned John of Gaunt's palace of the Savoy. Once again Richard saved the day; he met the rebels at Smithfield, and when the Mayor, William Walworth, struck down Tyler, promised to be himself their leader and redress their grievances, if they would go home. When the danger was over, however, the government ignored the King's promises; John Ball and thousands of the rebels were executed, and a period of savage repression followed. Yet the government had learned a lesson, and after the revolt the condition of the people slowly improved.

Chaucer must have witnessed these terrible events, for Mile End was not far from Aldgate, and the rebels poured through the gate below his house into the City. He may, indeed, have been in danger of his life, as a known dependant of John of Gaunt, yet his only mention of the revolt is in one of his last poems, *The Nun's Priest's Tale*, when the thieving fox is chased by the villagers:

> *Certes, he Jacke Straw and his meynee*
> *Ne made never shoutes half so shrille,*
> *Whan that they woulden any Fleming kille,*
> *As thilke day was made upon the fox.*

However, a few days after the revolt had been crushed in London, Chaucer sold the Thames Street house that he had inherited from his father. He was a good man of business, and it seems probable that these midsummer days of mob violence and destruction convinced him that London property was not a good investment.

Although John of Gaunt was not the power that he had been in Edward III's reign, Chaucer continued to prosper. He twice received a supplementary reward for his diligence as Controller, and shortly after the marriage of Richard II and Anne of Bohemia in January 1382, he was made Controller of the Petty Customs in the Port of London, evidently a sinecure, for he was allowed to have a permanent deputy. This was in addition to his other Controllership, and in this year a new and better custom house was built on 'the quay called the Wool Wharf', just west of the Tower.

At about this time he was translating the *De Consolatione Philosophiae* of Boethius, a distinguished sixth-century Roman who was thrown into prison for defending the liberties of his country. It was while awaiting death that he wrote his *Consolation of Philosophy*, a book that had an enormous influence in the Middle Ages, partly because he was thought to have been a Christian martyr, and revered accordingly as St Severinus. The book begins with Boethius bewailing his fate, which Chaucer translates: 'Hairs hoar be shed untimely upon mine head, and the slack skin trembleth of mine empty body . . . for

72

Fortune's Wheel. 'What other thing bewailen the cryings of tragedies but only the deeds of Fortune, that with an unwar stroke overturneth realms of great nobility?'

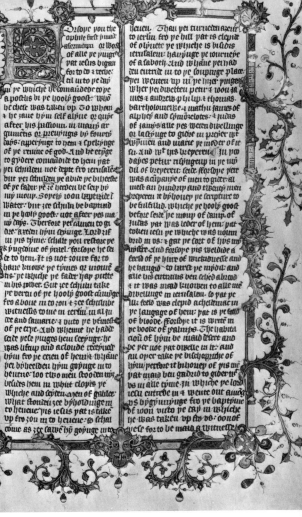

The Bible translated into English by Wycliffe and his disciples.

Fortune cloudy hath changed her deceivable cheer to me-ward.' Philosophy comes to console him, a goddess with burning eyes, who tells him that she knows that 'monster Fortune'. 'What other things bewail the cryings of tragedies,' she asks, 'but only the deeds of Fortune, that with an unware stroke overturneth realms of great nobility? . . . Yet, the last day of a man's life is a manner death to Fortune.' She goes on to discuss free will and predestination, managing to reconcile the two by showing that, though God foreknows man's actions, he does not determine them. The conclusion of the whole matter is that the gifts of Fortune are of little worth, and that true happiness is to be found only in God. Chaucer's medium was verse, and he can scarcely be called 'the father of English prose', yet his translation is important as illustrating the optimistic stoicism that he admired, and the philosophy of Boethius was to colour much of his later work.

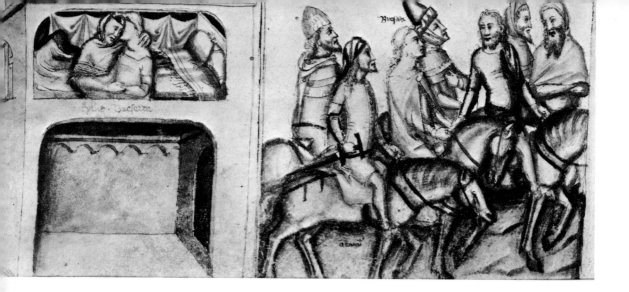

*Troilus and Criseyde*    It is apparent in his first great masterpiece; for it was during the troubled years after his translation of *Boethius*, when the young King was trying to assert his independence, and quarrelling with John of Gaunt, when Wycliffe and the Lollards were attacking the Papacy and abuses of the Church, that Chaucer wrote *Troilus and Criseyde*.

His source was Boccaccio's poem, *Il Filostrato*. Troilo, son of King Priam of Troy, falls in love with the young widow Criseida, whose father Calchas has deserted the city and joined the besieging Greeks. Troilo's friend Pandaro brings the lovers together, but their joy is cut short when the Trojans decide to send Criseida to her father, in exchange for one of their leaders, Antenor, a prisoner in the hands of the Greeks. Criseida swears to be true to Troilo, and to find a way of returning to Troy, but once in the Greek camp she soon succumbs to the blandishments of Diomede. Troilo seeks Diomede in battle, but is himself killed by Achilles.

In his version of the story, Chaucer professes to be no more than a translator. It is true that he generally follows Boccaccio's narrative closely, for the Italian was a brilliant story-teller, but he turns the *ottava rima* of the *Filostrato* into rhyme royal, sometimes alters the sequence of events and adds matter of his own; only about a third of his 8000 lines is strictly translation. The all-important change, however, is in the characters. Boccaccio's story is one of passionate lovers and commonplace seduction, but Chaucer's is the tragedy of a young man who plays the love-game according to courtly rules, with one who ultimately ignores them: of make-believe defeated by reality.

According to the convention, love refines the lover, and Troilus becomes the gentlest, bravest and noblest of knights, but, again according to the convention, when things go wrong, he has a tiresome way of swooning and taking to his

74

(*far left*) 'So gan the pain their heartes for to twiste.'

(*left*) 'This Diomed that led her by the bridle.'

Chaucer reading his poetry, probably *Troilus and Criseyde*, to a courtly company, which may include Richard II, Anne of Bohemia and John of Gaunt.

John Lydgate presenting one of his poems to the Earl of Salisbury. Lydgate (*c.* 1370–1449) was deeply indebted to his 'master Chaucer', his *Falls of Princes* being an expansion of the *Monk's Tale*, and *Story of Thebes* suggested by *Troilus and Criseyde*.

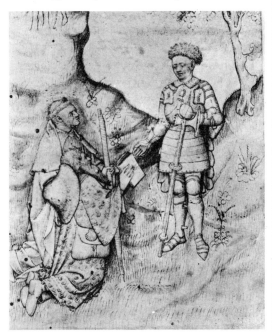

bed to die. He is too good to be true; but Criseyde is real flesh and blood: a well-meaning, affectionate, calculating, fickle – 'sliding of corage' – young lady, who plays up to Troilus, but is much more at home with her 'eem', her uncle Pandarus. And Pandarus is Chaucer's first great comic creation: a worldly, cynical, amiable jester, who good-naturedly seduces his niece on behalf of his friend, prodding her step by step towards his bed. Realism and real characters have entered English literature. Here is Pandarus beginning his seduction:

75

*With that she gan her eyen down to caste,*
*And Pandarus to coughe gan a lyte. . . .*

*'Now, my good eem, for Goddes love, I praye,'*
*Quod she, 'come off, and tell me what it is!' . . .*

*Criseyde, which that heard him in this wise,*
*Thought, 'I shall feele what he meaneth, y-wis.' . . .*

*Then fellen they in other tales glade,*
*Till at the last, 'O good eem,' quod she tho,*
*'For love of God, which that us bothe made,*
*Knows none of it but ye?' He saide, 'No.'*
*'Can he well speak of love?' quod she, 'I praye,*
*Tell me, for I the bet me shall purveye.*

*Then Pandarus a little gan to smile. . . .*

And he offers Criseyde advice on how to write a love letter:

*'Beblot it with thy teares eek a lyte;*
*And if thou write a goodly word all softe,*
*Though it be good, rehearse it not too ofte.'*

To rouse Troilus out of his despair, he bullies him and pulls his leg, 'comes leaping in', calls him a 'wretched mouse's heart', and with a final nudge, as Troilus approaches his bliss, whispers, 'If ye be wise, swooneth not now!'

When the sun has risen – 'O fool,' groans Troilus in Criseyde's arms, anticipating Donne's 'Busy old fool, unruly sun!' – Pandarus innocently asks Criseyde if she has slept well in spite of the rain. She blushes, calls him a fox, but soon begins to jest with him. But Troilus falls on his knees and thanks the best friend that ever was for bringing him to such bliss. Pandarus himself almost blushes, and with unconscious irony introduces the tragic theme:

*'Beware of this mischief:*
*That, thereas thou now brought art into blisse,*
*That thou thyself ne cause it not to misse.*

*For of Fortunes sharp adversity*
*The worste kind of infortune is this,*
*A man to have been in prosperity,*
*And it remembren when it passed is. . . .*

*Thou art at ease. . . .'*

The words are those of Boethius: his definition of tragedy.

'Then came she near, and set her down
upon the utterest corner of my bed.'
Boethius in his library and on the wall
a painting of himself in bed,
consoled by Philosophy.

The ominous word 'Fortune' introduces Book IV, and when Troilus hears that Criseyde is to go to the Greeks, he cries, 'Alas, Fortune!' complaining that he is now 'Wretch of wretches, out of honour fallen into misery', and in a long soliloquy, taken from Boethius, concludes that his tragedy was predestined, for if God foresees – 'purveys' – our thoughts as well as our deeds, 'we have no free choice':

'For if there mighte been a variance
To wrythen out from Goddes purveyinge,
There were no prescience of thing cominge.'

Which is the argument of Boethius with the goddess Philosophy, already translated by Chaucer: 'For if that they mighten wrythen away in other manner than they be purveyed, then should there be no steadfast prescience of thing to come.'

Troilus in real adversity is a much more credible and sympathetic character. His hopes and fears as he waits for Criseyde's promised return to Troy are poignantly described, and when Shakespeare, having read Chaucer's poem, wrote his play of *Troilus and Cressida*, his Troilus echoes the agonized cry of Chaucer's:

'O lady mine, Criseyde,
Where is your faith, and where is your beheste?
Where is your love? where is your truth?' he said.

77

A medieval scribe.

Chaucer dedicated his poem to 'moral Gower' and 'philosophical Strode', an Oxford scholar, and said farewell to the work that had occupied him so long:

*Go, little book, go little mine tragedye . . .*
*And for there is so great diversity*
*In English and in writing of our tongue,*
*So pray I God that none miswrite thee,*
*Ne thee mismetre for default of tongue,*
*And read whereso thou be, or elles sunge,*
*That thou be understond I God beseech!*

He had nothing to fear. *Troilus and Criseyde* was such a triumph that it helped to make the dialect in which it was written the standard speech of England, so that it can still be read with understanding and delight. From the Italians he had learned to create a structural whole instead of a medieval medley, and to this dramatic form he was able to add his own perfected manner of creating character: analyzing motive, telling us what his characters think, as well as what they say, and how they say it, so that in this great narrative poem he may be claimed as the father of the English drama and novel. Had he lived in the sixteenth century he would have rivalled Shakespeare in comedy and tragi-comedy; in the nineteenth he would have outranged Dickens.

Yet, after all, he had one thing to fear: careless 'miswriting'. Like any other author in the Middle Ages, before the invention of printing, he was dependent

Merton College, Oxford, of which the 'philosophical' Ralph Strode was a fellow. Merton was the first university college, founded 1274.

on professional scribes for the copying of his manuscripts. He had entrusted his recent works, *Boethius* and *Troilus*, to 'Adam, his owne scriveyne', ordering a number of copies of each, but on reading them he found them so full of errors that he had to spend precious time correcting and erasing. He was a patient and tolerant man, but even he was stung into protest by this mangling of his books, one of which, *Troilus*, he must have prized above all others, and half in earnest, half in jest, told Adam that if he made any more such careless copies, he deserved the scab in his scalp:

> *Adam, scriven, if ever it thee befalle*
> *Boece or Troilus to writen newe,*
> *Under thy long locks thou must have the scalle,*
> *But after my making thou write more true;*
> *So oft a-day I must thy work renewe,*
> *It to correct and eek to rub and scrape;*
> *And all is through thy negligence and rape.*

In 1383 Chaucer had been allowed to appoint a deputy for four months at the Wool Customs, and again for a month in 1384, to attend to his own urgent affairs, no doubt to get on with *Troilus*. Its writing in his spare time must have been a strain he would not care to repeat, and perhaps accounts for his successful application to appoint a permanent deputy in February 1385. He was forty-five, comfortably off, and could afford to take things more easily, and it may have been now that he moved across the river into the country, possibly to Greenwich,

*Justice of the Peace*

'Lo Greenwich! there many a shrew is in!'

for in October he was made one of the Justices of the Peace for Kent. He was a courtier and townsman, but now his travels about the county for quarter sessions would bring him into contact with country-folk and their affairs; with yeomen and ploughmen, millers, reeves and village parsons. Yet the new poem that he had in mind was curiously lacking in such earthy characters, nor was there another Pandarus to enliven it, nor another Criseyde; indeed, the poem was an apology, though a humorous one, for his having written the story of that faithless woman. Such a story was against all the rules of courtly love, according to which ladies are always faithful, and in *The Legend of Good Women* Chaucer returned to the old conventions, even introducing his tales of faithful women with a dream.

The Prologue begins with a defence of his passion for reading: old books are the storehouse of knowledge, and must be accepted as true unless proved to be false:

> *And as for me, though that my wit be lite,*
> *On bookes for to read I me delyte,*
> *And to them give I faith and full credence,*
> *And in mine heart have them in reverence*
> *So heartily, that there is game none*
> *That fro my bookes maketh me to goon,*
> *But it be seldom on the holiday;*
> *Save, certainly, when that the month of May*
> *Is comen, and that I hear the fowles singe,*
> *And that the flowres ginnen for to springe,*
> *Farewell my book and my devotion!*

May was the month of lovers in courtly poetry, but with Chaucer it appears to have been more than a convention. May really was his favourite month, and he describes the delights of living in the country in early summer, when the birds among the blossom on the branches sing praises to St Valentine. Another convention, however, had been introduced into French poetry, the Cult of the Daisy, and Chaucer makes charming play with this new game of make-believe, telling us how he gets up early to walk in the meadows to see the daisy

Picking daisies in May.

'Then love I most the flowres white and red, Such as men callen daysyes in our town.' ►

1402

open to the sun, and in the evening hurries back to see it close. The flower symbolizes a lady whom he professes to serve, and he complains that he has not sufficient 'English, rhyme or prose', to celebrate her worthily.

On the eve of the first of May he prepares to greet the flower next morning:

> *And, in a little arbour that I have,*
> *That benched was on turves fresh y-grave,*
> *I bade men shoulde me my couche make.*

He goes to sleep, and dreams that he is lying in the meadow, where he sees the God of Love approaching, 'and in his hand a queen', whose costume, green dress and white and gold crown, resembles a daisy. They are followed by another nineteen queens and innumerable ladies, all of whom were 'true of love', a sight that inspires him to write a *ballade* with the refraine, 'My lady cometh, that all this may distain.' The god sees Chaucer, and asks him:

> *'What dost thou here*
> *So nigh mine owne flower, so boldely?*
> *For it were better worthy, truely,*
> *A worm to nighen near my flower than thou.'*

When Chaucer humbly asks why, the god tells him that his 'translations' are directed against his service, that he holds it 'folly to serve love':

> *'Thou mayst it not denye;*
> *For in plain text, withouten need of glose,*
> *Thou hast translated the Romaunce of the Rose,*
> *That is an heresy against my lawe,*
> *And makest wise folk fro me withdrawe.*
> *And of Criseyde thou hast said as thee liste,*
> *That maketh men to women lesse truste,*
> *That ben as true as ever was any steel . . .*
> *If that thou live, thou shalt repenten this*
> *So cruelly, that it shall well be seen.'*

The daisy-like queen intercedes for Chaucer; the poor man, she tells the god, has written nothing in malice, and, after all, in his other poems he has done his best to serve the cause of love:

> *'Albeit that he cannot well endite,*
> *Yet hath he maked lewed folk delyte*
> *To serve you, in praising of your name.*
> *He made the book that hight the House of Fame,*

*And eek the Death of Blaunche the Duchesse,*
*And the Parlement of Foules as I guesse,*
*And all the love of Palamon and Arcite*
*Of Thebes, though the story is knowen lyte;*
*And many an hymne for your holidayes,*
*That highten ballades, roundels, virelayes;*
*And, for to speak of other holinesse,*
*He hath in prose translated Boece,*
*And made the Life also of Saint Cecile.'*

Chaucer kneels to thank the queen, at the same time protesting that he wrote about Criseyde to warn his readers against vice and infidelity. But the queen checks him sharply, and as a penance orders him to spend his time now in writing tales of faithful women, and the men

*'That all their life ne do not but assayen*
*How many women they may do a shame;*
*For in your world that is now held a game.'*

'In May, that mother is of
monthes glade,
That freshe flowres, blue and
white, and rede,
Be quick again.'

Eltham Palace, where Edward III entertained the Kings of France and Scotland.

It is a revealing Chaucerian comment on courtly love.

'And when this book is made,' the daisy-queen continues,

> '*give it the queen*
> *On my behalf, at Eltham or at Sheen.*'

Eltham, near Greenwich, was the favourite palace of Edward III, but Richard II and Anne of Bohemia preferred Sheen, twenty miles further up the river. The God of Love then adds:

> '*Hast thou not in a book, lieth in thy cheste,*
> *The greate goodness of the queen Alceste,*
> *That turned was into a dayesye?*'

Chaucer now recognizes the daisy-queen as Alcestis, whom, because of his 'little wit', he had failed to mention by name in the refrain of his *ballade*, and he promises to include her in his *Legend*. First, however, he is told to write, oddly enough, about Cleopatra:

> *And with that word my bookes gan I take,*
> *And right thus on my Legend gan I make.*

Lydgate tells us that Chaucer wrote *The Legend of Good Women* 'at the request of the queen'. At least he dedicated it to her, and it is even possible that she is the daisy-like Alcestis, whom he celebrates in such courtly fashion.

It may be that he already had two or three short stories of faithful women lying in his chest, and that his Prologue was a device for stringing them and

84

Penshurst Place, Kent:
the great hall, with the fire
in the middle.
Chaucer, as J.P. and
M.P. for Kent, must have
known the house,
built by Sir John Pulteney,
who made a fortune
out of financing
Edward III's French wars.

their successors together. He begins briskly with a brilliant description of a fourteenth-century sea-fight, which he calls the Battle of Actium, and vigorously taunts his faithless heroes: 'Have at thee, Jason!' 'Minos . . . now comest thou in the ring!' But by the time he had written another fifteen hundred lines he was groaning, 'It is so long, it were an heavy thing', and 'I am weary of him for to tell', and in his eighth tale he confessed that he was 'agroted', 'fed up', with writing endless stories on the same theme. He struggled through another three hundred lines, but finished in the middle of a sentence about Hypermnestra, his ninth good woman. He allowed himself, however, a parting jest:

> *Beware, ye women, of your subtle foe . . .*
> *And trusteth, as in love, no man but me.*

Chaucer's stories of good women are not among his best work, but the Prologue has a simplicity – though a simplicity that conceals much art – and freshness that make it one of the most engaging things he ever wrote. And metrically *The Legend* is important, as the first poem to be written in heroic couplets.

'And heaterly they hurtlen all at ones,
And from the top down come the greate stones,
In goeth the grapenel so full of crooks;
Among the ropes run the shearing hooks.
In with the pole-axe presseth he and he;
Behind the mast beginneth he to flee,
And out again, and driveth him overboard.'

86

There were reasons other than boredom that could have led to Chaucer's unchivalrous abandonment of his good women. By 1386 the affairs of England were in such a sorry plight that the French were assembling prefabricated forts in preparation for an invasion, and there was no united government to repel them. Richard, an extravagant and unstable young man, was trying to govern through favourites. In opposition was a baronial party, now led by another of his uncles, the Duke of Gloucester, for in March John of Gaunt had resumed his search for castles in Spain. Parliament met in October, among its members being Geoffrey Chaucer, one of the Knights of the Shire for Kent. Gloucester and his party at once attacked the King's friends, some of whom were executed, some imprisoned, while others fled the country. Richard managed to reassert himself for a time, but by the beginning of 1388 Gloucester and his party, the Lords Appellant, supported by the 'Merciless' Parliament, were in control.

What part Chaucer took in these proceedings is unknown, but we catch a fascinating glimpse of him, and almost hear his voice, when on 15 October 1386 he was called as a witness in the High Court of Chivalry in the suit between Sir Richard Scrope and Sir Robert Grosvenor, as to the right to the

arms, *Azure, a bend Or.* 'Geoffrey Chaucer, Esquire, of the age of 40 years and
• upwards, armed for 27 years'. that is, since his French campaign of 1359, gave
evidence for Scrope.

> 'He had seen them armed in France before the town of Retters . . . and the
> said Sir Richard in the entire arms . . . during the whole expedition, till the
> said Geoffrey was taken.'

Asked whether he had ever heard of any claim of Grosvenor to bear the arms,
he replied:

> 'No, but said that he was once in Friday Street, London, and, as he was
> walking in the street, he saw a new sign made of the said arms, hanging out;
> and he asked what inn it was that had hung out these arms of Scrope? And
> one answered him: No, sir; they are not hung out as the arms of Scrope, but
> they are painted and put there by a knight of the county of Chester, whom
> men call Sir Robert Grosvenor. And that was the first time that he had ever
> heard speak of Sir Robert Grosvenor.'

Scrope won his case, and Grosvenor had to wear his arms with a difference.

*Semi-retirement*      Now that John of Gaunt was out of the country, and his younger brother
and rival, Gloucester, in power, Chaucer may have suffered for his connection with the House of Lancaster. His colleague at the Customs, for
example, Sir Nicholas Brembre, a former Mayor of London but one of Lancaster's supporters, was hanged. He himself was not re-elected to Parliament.
On the other hand, John of Gaunt's son Henry, Earl of Derby, one of the
Lords Appellant, might well have defended the poet's interests, and in July
1387 he seems to have been sent with Sir William Beauchamp on a mission to
Calais. Yet, in that for him momentous month of October 1386 he surrendered
the Aldgate house in which he had lived for some twelve years and written
most of his poetry, and in December he either resigned or was dismissed from
both his Controllerships. This meant a considerable loss of income, and when
Philippa died a year later, her pension was lost as well. He still had his annuity
of £10 from John of Gaunt, but the sale of his two royal annuities of twenty
marks each, and the issue of writs for his arrest for debt, suggest that he was
short of ready money in 1388. If so, his triple *ballade* to *Fortune*, with the refrain,
'For finally, Fortune, I thee defy!' may belong to this lean period, as also the
beautiful, nostalgic *Former Age*.

In the two years 1385–7 his way of life had been completely changed: instead
of being a married man working in London as a busy government official, he
was now a country gentleman and a widower, with a reduced income, but far
more leisure. Perhaps, after all, his complete withdrawal from the Customs was

The House of Lords in Chaucer's time: bishops on the right of the throne where the King sat, nobles on the left.

John of Gaunt entertained by King John of Portugal.

deliberate. If he was living in Greenwich, he had seen bands of pilgrims, men and women of all ages and every station in life, riding on their way to Canterbury to visit the shrine in the cathedral, where Thomas à Becket had been murdered two hundred years before. Philomela, Phyllis, Hypermnestra and the rest of his good women, even Alcestis herself, whose story he had not yet reached, bored him, but the Prologue to his *Legend*, combined with the sight of pilgrims, was an inspiration. Why not write a series of stories told by a heterogeneous company of Canterbury pilgrims, introducing them in another Prologue, and linking their tales with talk on the way? And, perhaps in the spring of 1387, perhaps on 16 April, he began to write:

Pilgrim's badge, from the Shrine of St Thomas.

> *Whan that April with his showres soote*
> *The drought of March hath pierced to the roote,*
> *And bathed every vein in such licour,*
> *Of which virtue engendred is the flour . . .*
> *Then longen folk to goon on pilgrimages.*

It was true: a pilgrimage was a pleasant sort of holiday, probably with interesting companions, and cheaper than ordinary travel, for a pilgrim might expect a certain amount of hospitality on the way, and at the end there was the satisfaction of absolution, of knowing that his sins had been forgiven.

*The pilgrims*

In the Middle Ages pilgrimages were often imposed by priestly confessors as a penance, but by Chaucer's time the whole system had become commercialized. As early as the year 1300 the Papacy became a sort of travel agency to attract tourists, when the Pope offered plenary indulgences to all those who made a pilgrimage to Rome that year. A century later a trip to Rome was advertised as being as efficacious as the longer journey to Jerusalem, and the

A fourteenth-century map,
showing the Pilgrims' Way:
London–Rochester–Canterbury.

The two main centres of medieval pilgrimage: (below, left) Rome, and
Jerusalem: Church of the Holy Sepulchre.

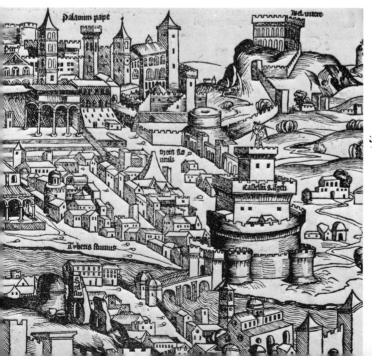

'Our liege lordes seal on my patente.'
Reading a fabricated Papal Bull in Canter-bury Cathedral.
These papal edicts took their name from the seal: Latin *bulla*.

pilgrim was told how to make best use of his time: a prayer on one of the steps of St Peter's earned seven years' pardon; but this was scarcely worth the breath: a visit to Rome during the summer season secured a reprieve of fourteen thousand years from purgatorial pains. Then, there were professional pilgrims, or palmers, who begged their way from shrine to shrine, their hats and cloaks stuck with badges of the holy places they had visited; and a sinner who could not, or would not, make the journey, might hire a palmer to go to some holy place to obtain for him a vicarious absolution.

The sale of relics was a profitable side-line, and pardoners, papal agents who travelled the country, did a brisk traffic in pigs' bones and indulgences. The trade was not confined to the Papacy, and while Chaucer was writing, the nave of Canterbury Cathedral was being rebuilt in the Perpendicular style with money received from the sale of forty-day indulgences issued by Arch-bishop Sudbury. No wonder Wycliffe and the Lollards so bitterly denounced pilgrimages and their attendant abuses. But what a subject for Chaucer!

It is not suggested that all the pilgrims whom, in imagination, Chaucer met in the Tabard Inn on that memorable April evening, and accompanied from Southwark to Canterbury, were going for any other reason than to pay homage to England's most famous saint and martyr. Chaucer tells us that he himself was preparing to go 'with full devout corage', and no doubt so too were the poor Parson, his brother the Ploughman, the Knight and one or two of the others, but devoutness of disposition is not easy to detect in, say, the Miller and Reeve, or even in the Monk and Friar.

92

The nave of Canterbury Cathedral, which was being rebuilt when Chaucer's pilgrims visited it. ▶

Nun and friar in the stocks.

*(left)* London – Rochester – Canterbury – Dover.
A thirteenth-century guide.

'And forth we riden a little more than pace.'
Pilgrims on the road. ▶

Making beds at an inn.

Pilgrims at an inn.

Chaucer was very careful to make his pilgrims representative of contemporary society, and it is worth pausing to consider his selection of characters. In his time the clergy were relatively far more numerous than they are today: the Oxford Clerk, Summoner and Pardoner, for example, would all be in minor orders. Thus, assuming that the Prioress had only one attendant priest, there are nine representatives of the clergy, and, excluding Chaucer for the moment, nineteen laymen, seven of whom are countrymen, eleven townsmen, and one a sailor. The countrymen range from the Knight and his son the Squire, also a representative of the courtly school of love, to the Reeve and Ploughman, while

of the town-dwellers there are five wealthy Gildsmen, a Merchant, a business-woman and two professional men: a Lawyer and a Doctor. Three of the company are women: the Prioress, her Nun, and the Wife of Bath, who is also something of a professional pilgrim, for not only has she visited the shrines at Boulogne, Cologne and Compostella, but she has also been to Rome, and no less than three times to Jerusalem: 'She knew much of wandering by the way.'

By this time the laity had little respect for the clergy, apart from the humble parsons, who for a mere pittance ministered to their flocks. Wycliffe, who had died in 1384, had voiced the hostility of the layman to the wealth and power of the Church, in both politics and its ecclesiastical courts, as well as to its encouragement of superstition and other abuses. When in 1377 there were two Popes, one in Rome and a rival one in Avignon, the Papacy fell into even greater disrepute. Bishops, as a whole, were worldly and ambitious, little con-cerned with spiritual affairs; but it was against the regular clergy, those living according to rules, that the layman's animosity was chiefly directed. The monks had forgotten their original functions as teachers and custodians of learning, and now lived easy and useless lives within their monasteries, which had acquired vast wealth and estates on which they kept their tenants in serfdom. Even more disliked were the friars, who had long abandoned their asceticism and poverty, and toured the country preaching and begging, selling absolution as they went, and squeezing a last farthing from a needy widow. Parish priests detested these parasites, who robbed them of their living, even more than monks and friars detested one another, and friars of one order their rivals of the other three.

The twenty-ninth pilgrim, unrecognized by his companions, was Chaucer himself, a man of forty-seven, of far more varied experience than any of the others, and acquainted with all manner of people, from the King and John of Gaunt to apprentices and carters, and with an enviably wide circle of friends, English and foreign, that included ambassadors, merchants, poets and men of letters: among them Sir Edward Berkeley, John Gower, Ralph Strode, Sir Henry Scogan, Jean Froissart and Eustache Deschamps. The son of a London vintner, he was both townsman and countryman, a courtier, soldier, diplomat and civil servant, a Justice of the Peace and former Member of Parliament. He had fought in Flanders, and travelled in France and Italy, where he had seen the beginnings of the Renaissance, and there can have been few Englishmen so widely read as he. Among the ancients, Ovid, Virgil, Statius and Boethius were his constant companions; he had devoured everything worth reading in English, and in French, from Lorris and Meun to Machault, Froissart and Deschamps, while in Italian he had read Dante, Petrarch and Boccaccio. Moreover, he was a student of the Bible and the early Fathers, as well as of

96

The Shrine of St Thomas was destroyed at the Reformation, but its representation survives in the thirteenth-century stained glass of Canterbury Cathedral.

The martyrdom of Thomas à Becket, Archbishop of Canterbury, 1170.

astronomy, astrology, alchemy and other medieval sciences. Yet, much as he loved books, he loved men far more. Their infinite variety of appearance and manner, their idiosyncrasies, foibles and follies, virtues and even vices, were for him a source of wonder and perpetual delight, rarely of aversion and disgust. Unlike Wycliffe, he was no dedicated reformer, but he was a poet who could most vividly record his impressions, and with humorous irony slyly expose to ridicule the abuses that others denounced. He was sociable and a very good mixer, but his quiet, diffident and courteous manner was deceptive, for though he spoke to each of the other pilgrims before they went to bed, we may be sure that he had encouraged them to speak far more to him, so that each was a life-like portrait imprinted in that shrewd, retentive mind, soon to be developed into imperishable verse.

His imaginary companions were an old-fashioned, courteous Knight, accompanied by his son, a young Esquire, and a Yeoman; an affected, senti-mental Prioress with her attendant Nun and Priest and pampered dogs; a hunting Monk, whose sleeves were trimmed with finest fur; an ingratiating Friar; a bragging Merchant; a shy Oxford Clerk; a wary Lawyer; an epicurean Franklin; five wealthy Gildsmen and their drunken Cook; a piratical Shipman; an abstemious Doctor; a jolly, bold-faced Widow of Bath; a poor, con-scientious Parson and his brother, a Ploughman; a muscular, ribald Miller; a cunning Manciple; a choleric old Reeve; a scabby, lecherous Summoner, and a plausible, shrill-voiced Pardoner. Finally, there was their host, Harry Bailly, landlord of the Tabard, a big, jovial man, though one not entirely happy in his married life. Mrs Bailly was not there to welcome her guests, but her

'As Newton numbered the stars, and as Linnaeus numbered the plants, so Chaucer numbered the classes of men.'
William Blake's vision of the Canterbury Pilgrims leaving the Tabard Inn.

'All his fantasye
Was turned for to learn astrologye.'

'Great cheere made our Host us everyone,
And to the supper set he us anon,
And served us with vitaille at the beste.'

husband has something to say later about that formidable termagant, and, incidentally, about the treatment of the Tabard servants:

> 'By Goddes bones! when I beat my knaves,
> She bringth me forth the greate clobbed staves,
> And crieth, "Slay the dogges everyone,
> And break them, bothe back and every bone!"
> And if that any neighebor of mine
> Will not in churche to my wife incline,
> Or be so hardy to her to trespace,
> When she comth home she rampeth in my face,
> And crieth, "False coward, wreak thy wife!
> By corpus bones, I will have thy knife,
> And thou shalt have my distaff and go spinne!"'

We can understand why Harry Bailly offered to be the pilgrims' guide to Canterbury, and master of their revels. Each of the twenty-nine, he ruled, was to tell four tales, two on the way to Canterbury, two on the way back, and he who told the best was to be given a supper at the Tabard on their return.

Never before in English literature had there been anything like this company of real, unidealized, contemporary men and women; and there was to be nothing comparable again until Shakespeare began to write two hundred years later. It is true that realism was creeping into the visual arts and into the religious drama, in the robust comic relief of the miracle plays; and in Chaucer's own work, from *The Book of the Duchess* to *Troilus and Criseyde*, we can trace his growing impatience with make-believe, and the emergence of his genius for dramatic realism; but now he shattered the barrier of medieval conventions, and leaped at a bound into the world of modern literature.

It was characteristic so cheerfully to set himself the impossible task of writing nearly a hundred and twenty tales, one for every mile of the journey to Canterbury and back, but his time was now his own, and he already had a few stories that he could allocate to suitable characters: *Palamon and Arcite* to the Knight, and *The Life of St Cecilia* to the Nun; and, inspired by his new theme and his less respectable characters, he began to write a bawdy story for the Miller. He prefaced it, however, with a repetition of the apology that he had already made in his *Prologue*:

> For Goddes love, deemeth not that I say
> Of evil intent, but for I must rehearse
> Their tales alle, be they bettre or worse,
> Or elles falsen some of my mattere.

*The Canterbury Tales* were to occupy Chaucer for the rest of his life, though not without interruptions. His newly won leisure did not last long. His mission to Calais in July 1387 may have lasted a year, and in July 1389 he was appointed Clerk of the King's Works, responsible for the maintenance and repair of the Palace of Westminster, Tower of London, Eltham, Sheen and other royal buildings. It was a post for which he was well qualified by his experience at the Wool Customs, for though his deputy and subordinates attended to the detail, he was responsible for the book-keeping and finance, which involved large sums. A few months later he was made one of the five commissioners who were to inspect and organize repair of the banks of the Thames between Woolwich and Greenwich. Nor was this all; in the summer of 1390 he was ordered to superintend the repair of St George's Chapel in Windsor Castle, when he was already supervising the erection of wooden stands at Smithfield, from which the King and Queen could watch the jousts that were to be held there.

These new appointments and activities may have been in some measure due to Richard's assertion of his authority in May 1389, the consequent decline of the power of Gloucester and the other Appellants, and the return from Spain in November of John of Gaunt, who now reconciled himself and his son Henry with the King. In any event, Chaucer was very busy at this time, and *The Canterbury Tales* can have made little progress. There was yet another call upon his time. As Clerk of the King's Works, he sometimes had to carry large sums of money about with him, and evidently his movements were closely watched, for in September 1390 he was attacked and robbed three times within four days. The first occasion was at 'Foul Oak' in Kent, where he lost £20 of the King's money, his horse and other valuables. Three days later he was robbed twice: first at Westminster, then at Hatcham in Surrey, when another £20 was taken. The thieves were caught, and Chaucer was absolved from repayment of the government money, but the case dragged on for several months, and he had to spend valuable time in attendance at the law courts.

Highway robbery in the Middle Ages.

Westminster Hall (*far left*), rebuilt by Richard II. As Clerk of the King's Works, Chaucer was responsible for its maintenance. Chaucer was also responsible for the erection of stands (*above*) from which the King could watch jousting, and for the repair of St George's Chapel, Windsor (*left*).

103

'Thine astrolabe hath a ring to putten on the thumb of thy right hand in taking the height of things.'
A thirteenth-century English astrolabe: 'so noble an instrument'.

This may well have proved the last straw. For two years his official duties had seriously interfered with his writing, and in June 1391 he exchanged his post as Clerk of the Works for that of Deputy Forester of North Petherton, near Taunton, a far less exacting office, involving only the general administration of the royal property. He would now be able to resume *The Canterbury Tales* with little interruption, and even found time to write *A Treatise of the Astrolabe*, a simple account of a complex astronomical instrument, for his ten-year-old son Lewis. The introduction is charming:

Little Lewis my son, I have perceived well by certain evidences thine ability to learn sciences touching numbers and proportions; and as well consider I thy busy prayer in special to learn the Treatise of the Astrolabe. Then, for as much as a philosopher saith, 'he wrappeth him in his friend, that condescendeth to the prayers of his friend,' therefore have I given thee a sufficient Astrolabe as for our horizon, constructed after the latitude of Oxford; upon which, by mediation of this little treatise, I purpose to teach thee a certain number of conclusions appertaining to the same instrument.

I say a certain [number] of conclusions, for three causes. The first cause is this: trust well that all the conclusions that have been found, or else possibly might be found in so noble an instrument as an Astrolabe, be unknown perfectly to any mortal man in this region, as I suppose. Another cause is this: that soothly, in any treatise of the Astrolabe that I have seen, there be some conclusions that will not in all things perform all they promise; and some of them be too hard to thy tender age of ten year to conceive.

This treatise, divided in five parts, will I show thee under full light rules and naked words in English; for Latin ne canst thou yet but small, my little son. . . . And Lewis, if so be that I show thee in my light English as true conclusions touching this matter, and not only as true but as many and as subtle conclusions as be shown in Latin in any common treatise of the Astrolabe, con [give] me the more thank. . . . But consider well, that I ne usurp [claim] not to have found this work of my labour or of mine engin [skill]. I n'am but a lewd [unlearned] compilator of the labour of old astrologers, and have it translated in mine English only for thy doctrine.

'A forester was he, soothly, as I guesse.'

Little is known about Chaucer's children, but the Lewis Chaucer who was one of the squires in the garrison of Carmarthen Castle in 1403 was probably the Lewis of the *Astrolabe*. With him was Thomas Chaucer, who had been in the service of John of Gaunt, and became Forester of North Petherton. It is almost certain that he too was Geoffrey's son, for he used the same seal, and when he died after a distinguished career, the arms of the poet's wife, Philippa Roet, were depicted on his tomb, along with those of his cousins the Beauforts, and other aristocratic relations. There was also an Elizabeth Chaucer, towards whose expenses John of Gaunt contributed £50 when she entered the Abbey of Barking as a novice. Such a princely sum is understandable if Elizabeth were the niece of his mistress Katherine Swynford, whom he had always loved dearly, and by whom he had four children, who were given the name of Beaufort. In 1396, shortly after the death of his second wife, Constance of Castile, he married Katherine, so that Chaucer thus became his brother-in-law, and uncle of his son Henry, who was soon to become Henry IV.

It was probably in 1393 that Chaucer wrote a humorous poem to his friend Sir Henry Scogan, protesting that his breaking the rules of courtly love by deserting his lady had caused the pestilential rains that autumn, and might lead Cupid to forsake old men 'of our figure . . . hoar and round of shape, That be so likely folk in love to speed.' It was no good dismissing his warning with, 'Lo! Olde Grisel list to rhyme and playe!' for the grey-haired old man's muse was asleep; but, he added in the envoy:

> *Scogan, that kneelest at the streames head*
> *Of grace, of all honour and worthinesse,*
> *In the end of which stream I am dull as dead,*
> *Forgot in solitary wildernesse. . . .*

Scogan was upstream at the Court of Windsor, Chaucer downstream at Greenwich, and he asked his friend to put in a word for him 'where it may fructify'. It seems probable that Scogan did, for in February 1394 the King awarded Chaucer another annuity of £20.

He still drew his salary as Forester of North Petherton, and should have been comfortably off, but his occasional borrowings from the Exchequer and elsewhere make it clear that he was still sometimes short of ready money. But payments due to him were often in arrears, and he probably borrowed only in anticipation of their receipt. Again, when a widow, Isabella Buckholt, sued him for a debt of £14 in 1398, it must have been an old claim dating back to the time when her husband was employed by Chaucer when Clerk of the King's Works. He did not pay, for the King gave him letters of protection and, in reply to his request, a butt of wine each year for the remainder of his life.

Thomas Chaucer (d. 1434) and his wife. Their only child, Alice, married the Duke of Suffolk. ▶
Brass on the altar tomb of St Mary, Ewelme, Oxfordshire.

This was a critical time for Richard II. After nine years of constitutional government, he suddenly turned on his old opponents, the Appellants; Gloucester was murdered, another executed, and the remaining three banished, one of them being John of Gaunt's son Henry. Then, when John of Gaunt died early in 1399, Richard seized all the wide estates of Lancaster. In July Henry returned to England to claim his inheritance, and by September Richard was his prisoner in the Tower, where, on the 29th, he signed a deed of abdication, and on the next day the new Duke of Lancaster was proclaimed King as Henry IV.

Chaucer lost no time in sending his congratulations and *A Complaint*, a mock *ballade* addressed to his 'lady dear', his empty purse, with the refrain, 'Be heavy again, or elles must I die,' and *envoy*:

> *O conquerour of Brutes Albioun!*
> *Which that by line and free electioun*
> *Be very king, this song to you I sende;*
> *And ye, that mayen all our harm amende,*
> *Have mind upon my supplicatioun!*

By return came the reply of 'England's conqueror': confirmation of Richard's annuity of £20 and yearly butt of wine, with an additional annuity of forty marks. Perhaps it was this windfall that persuaded Chaucer to leave Greenwich and return to London, where on 24 December he rented a house in the garden of Westminster Abbey.

'Hec indentura . . . Galfrido Chaucers armigero unum tenementum . . . situatum in gardino capelle.'
Chaucer's lease of a Westminster house, Christmas Eve 1399.

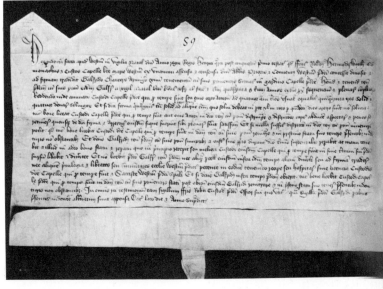

Richard II (1367–1400)
and his beloved wife
Anne of Bohemia (d. 1394).

'Here, cousin, seize the crown;
On this side my hand, and on that side yours.'
Richard II surrenders the crown to Henry Bolingbroke.

He was nearly sixty, an old man in those days, and though, with charac- teristic optimism, he had taken a fifty-three-year lease of his new house, he must have known that he could not expect to live much longer. It was Christmas 1399, but for the last twelve years he had lived in that magical week in April when he had begun his imaginary pilgrimage with Harry Bailly of the Tabard and his guests. Of his hundred and sixteen projected tales, he had written only twenty-three, and some of these were unfinished, and the pilgrims were only just approaching Canterbury. It was time to round off what he had done with a moral story, and complete the talk with which he linked the tales. As he put them together in his Westminster house, he must have re-read them with delight, modestly marvelling, perhaps, at what he had created, and at the range of his achievement: characters from every walk of life, stories of every age, from Greek mythology to his own time, tragic tales and tales of the broadest bawdy. . . .

'I Henry of Lancaster challenge this Realm of England and the Crown.'
Coronation of Henry IV, 1399.

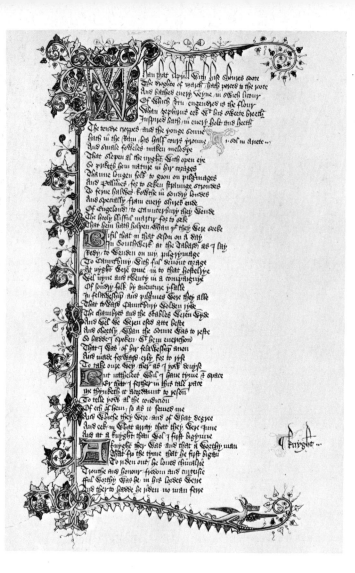

'Whan that Aprill with hise
      shoures soote
The droghte of march hath perced
      to the roote. . . .'
The beginning of the Prologue to
*The Canterbury Tales*: from the
illuminated Ellesmere manuscript.

*A-morrow, whan that day began to springe,*
*Up rose our Host, and was our aller cock,*
*And gathered us together, all in a flock,*
*And forth we riden,*

led by the Miller, who plays them out of Southwark on his bagpipes, the unsociable Reeve bringing up the rear.

As is only proper, the Knight tells the first story, that of the friends and cousins, Palamon and Arcite, who become rivals for the love of Emily, the young sister-in-law of King Theseus. There are splendid descriptive passages, notably that of the Temple of Mars, promised many years before in *Anelida and*

'A Knight ther was.'    'The Miller was a stout carl.'    'The Reeve, a slender choleric man.'

*Arcite*, and lines of astonishing compression: Hypocrisy, for example, as 'The smiler with the knife under the cloak.' Arcite defeats Palamon in battle, but is mortally injured in a fall from his horse, and dies in his lady's arms:

> *'What is this world? what asketh men to have?*
> *Now with his love, now in his colde grave*
> *Alone, withouten any company.'*

It was, all the pilgrims agreed, 'a noble story', but Robin the Miller, already very drunk, insists that he has an even nobler one: about the cuckolding of a carpenter. The Reeve is a carpenter, and angrily tells him to stint his clap and stop his drunken harlotry; but there is no stopping the Miller and his story of the Oxford student's frolic with the carpenter's wanton poppet. The Reeve is furious, but, full of self-pity, begins to moralize, until cut short by the Host, who points out that it is already seven-thirty, that they have passed Deptford and are approaching Greenwich, where so many undesirable characters – such as Chaucer, presumably – live. The Reeve more than gets his own back in his story of two north-country Cambridge students and a dishonest Miller, closely resembling Robin, whose wife and daughter are both served like the carpenter's pigsny. The Cook thinks this the funniest story he has ever heard, claws the Reeve on his back, and cries, 'God forbid that we should stop at this,' and insists on telling his story of a London apprentice. However, he gets only as far as his hero's dimissal, and removal to the house of a friend, who

> *had a wife that held for countenance*
> *A shop, and swyved for her sustenance.*

111

Chaucer with the manuscript of *The Canterbury Tales*.

'A Cook to boil the chicknes.'

'Of this Cokes tale maked Chaucer na more,' the scribe sedately noted in his manuscript. No wonder. Chaucer must have felt that three gross stories in succession, however amusing, were too much of a good thing: that his Canter-bury Tales were degenerating into bawdy-house stories. Or perhaps the Cook is stopped by the arrival of the pilgrims at Dartford, where presumably they spend the night.

It is ten o'clock, 18 April, before the tales are resumed, when the Host asks the Man of Law for one. The lawyer agrees, but apologizes for his lack of new and profitable matter, for that fellow

> *Chaucer, though he can but lewedly*
> *On metres and on rhyming craftily,*
> *Hath said them in such English as he can*
> *Of olde time, as knoweth many a man;*
> *And if he have not said them, deare brother,*
> *In one book, he hath said them in another.*

On the other hand, it has to be admitted that he has not written any wicked tales of unnatural abominations, such as incest. Chaucer cannot resist a dig at his old friend Gower, who, no doubt objecting to the new realism, was never-theless writing just such 'wicked examples' in his *Confessio Amantis*. 'Of such cursed stories I say *fie!*' exclaims the Man of Law, as he begins to tell the impeccably moral story of Constance. And very beautifully he tells this old romance of the long-suffering Roman princess, among the conventional apparatus of which the one passage of contemporary realism stands out with startling clarity:

Pilgrims' badges.

112

Sergeant of the Lawe.'    'A Shipman, dwelling far by west.'    ' A Prioresse, full simple and coy.'

> *Have ye not seen sometime a pale face*
> *Among a press, of him that hath been lad*
> *Toward his death, where-as him got no grace,*
> *And such a colour in his face hath had*
> *Men mighte know the face that was bestad*
> *Amonges all the faces in that rout:*
> *So stands Constance, and looketh her about.*

Harry Bailly is so impressed that he rises in his stirrups and cries, 'This was a thrifty tale!' Then,

> 'Sir Parish Priest,' quod he, 'for Goddes bones,
> Tell us a tale, as was thy foreword yore.
> I see well that ye learned men in lore
> Can muche good, by Goddes dignitee!'
> The Parson him answered 'Benedicite!
> What aileth the man so sinfully to swear?'
> Our Host answered, 'O Jankin, be ye there?
> I smell a Lollard in the wind,' quod he . . .
> 'This Lollard here will preachen us somewhat.'
> 'Nay, by my father's soul! that shall he nat,'
> Saide the Shipman, 'here shall he nat preache.'

So, lest the pilgrims should be corrupted by the words of a reforming parson, the pirate tells his tale of the ingenious monk who borrows a hundred francs from his friend, with which to seduce his wife.

The Prioress then tells her sentimental, unpleasant little anti-semitic tale, and, after a suitable pause, the Host takes notice of Chaucer for the first time:

113

Explicit

heere biginneth Chaucers tale of melibee

And saide thus, 'What man art thou?' quod he;
Thou lookest as thou wouldest find an hare,
For ever upon the ground I see thee stare.

'Approache near, and look up merrily.
Now ware you, sirs, and let this man have place!
He in the waist is shape as well as I;
This were a poppet in an arm t'embrace
For any woman, small and fair of face.
He seemeth elvish by his countenance,
For unto no wight doth he dalliance.
'Say now somewhat, since other folk have said;
Tell us a tale of mirth, and that anon.'
'Hoste,' quod I, 'be not ill satisfied,
For other tale certes know I none,
But of a rhyme I learned long agone.'
'Yea, that is good,' quod he; 'now shall we heare
Some dainty thing, me thinketh, by his cheere.'

'What man art thou?'

Chaucer's dainty thing is *The Rhyme of Sir Thopas*, a burlesque of the popular romances of his day:

> Sir Thopas wax a doughty swain,
> White was his face as paindemain,
>   His lippes red as rose;
> His colour like scarlet in grain,
> And I you tell in good certain,
>   He had a seemly nose.

114

'A Monk ther was, that loved venerie;
Full many a dainty horse had he in stable;
Greyhounds he had as swift as fowl in flight;
Of pricking and of hunting for the hare
Was all his lust, for no cost would he spare.'

After a hundred lines of this the Host roars,

'No more of this, for Goddes dignitee! . . .
Mine eares achen of thy drasty speeche . . .'
'Why so?' quod I, 'why wilt thou hinder me
More of my tale than any other man,
Since that it is the beste rhyme I can?'
'By God,' quod he, 'for plainly, at a word,
Thy drasty rhyming is not worth a turd . . .
Sir, at a word, thou shalt no longer rhyme . . .
So tell in prose somewhat at the least
In which there be some mirth or some doctrine.'
'Gladly,' quod I, 'by Goddes sweete paine
I will you tell a little thing in prose.'

This turns out to be a debate between Melibeus and his wife Prudence, on the
rival merits of vengeance and pardon. Innumerable proverbs and axioms of the
best authorities are quoted, and this 'little thing in prose' must have taken
Chaucer some two hours to deliver. The joke seems to be that the pilgrims
listen attentively to 'this merry tale', as he calls it, especially the Host, who
ruefully compares the gentle Prudence with his own wife, so 'big in arms',
waiting for him at the Tabard.

But they are approaching Rochester, and he turns to the Monk, urging him,
with bawdy banter about his sexual potentialities, to tell a tale. The Monk is
surprisingly patient, promises to relate a number of 'tragedies', and proceeds to
give short encyclopaedic accounts of those who have 'fallen out of high degree
into misery'. Among them is the tragedy of Bernabo Visconti, whom Chaucer
had visited in Milan, but after a score of these brief lives the Knight exclaims:
'Ho! Good sir, no more of this!' And the Host dutifully echoes him: 'No

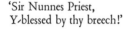

'Sir Nunnes Priest,
Y-blessed by thy breech!'

'A Doctor of Physic.'

'. . . Thine urinals,
God bless them, and
our Lady Saint Marie!'
A physician, possibly
John of Gaddesden.

more! Thy talking is not worth a butterfly.' Only the clinking of the bells on the Monk's bridle has kept him awake, he protests: 'Say, somewhat of hunting.' But the Monk turns sulky, and the Host appeals to the Prioress's attendant Priest.

*The Nun's Priest's Tale* is one of the very best things that Chaucer ever wrote: the transformation of the old fable of Reynard the Fox into a gay mock-heroic story of Chanticleer the cock and his favourite hen, Partlet, who debate in high style the significance of dreams. Few writers can describe movement with such vivid brevity as Chaucer:

> He looketh as it were a grim lioun,
> And on his toes he roameth up and doun,
> Him deigned not to set his foot to grounde;
> He chucketh when he hath a corn y-founde,
> And to him runnen then his wives alle.

And again, the chase of the fox that is carrying off poor Chanticleer:

> Ran cow and calf and eke the very hogges,
> So were they feared by barking of the dogges
> And shouting of the men and women eek:
> They ranne so they thought their hearte breake.
> They yelleden as fiendes doon in helle;
> The duckes cryden as men would them kille;
> The geese for feare flew over the trees. . . .

116

With good-natured obscenity the Host thanks the Priest, and, as they ride into Rochester for the night, perhaps makes a mental note that this is the winning story so far.

Next morning the Doctor of Physic's pathetic little story of Virginia, slain by her father for love, so moves the Host that he calls on God to protect the Doctor's urinals and jordans, before calling on the Pardoner for his tale. The

Seal and map of the City of Rochester, showing the Norman castle.

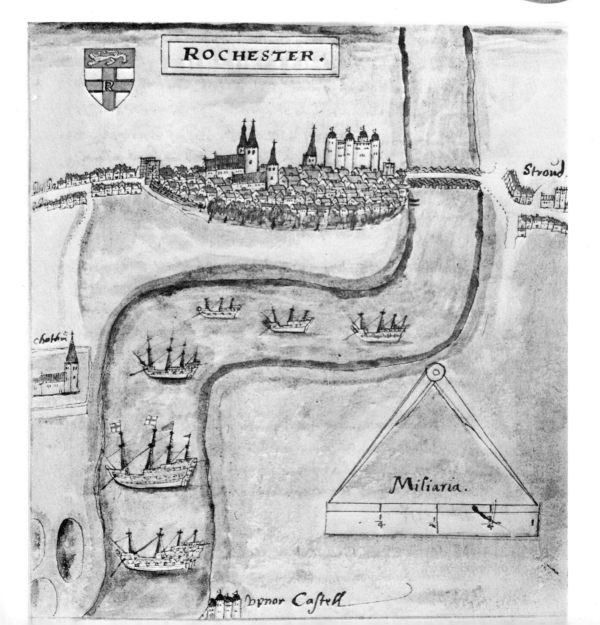

'A gentil Pardoner . . .
His wallet bretful of pardon.'

'A good Wife . . . of beside Bath;
Bold was her face.'

gentlefolk demur, expecting some ribaldry, but the Pardoner promises them
'some honest thing' when he has slaked his thirst at the neighbouring ale-house.
He is already drunk enough to boast how he makes a hundred marks a year –
as much as Chaucer ever earned – by his tricks and exploitation of his listeners'
greed. He then inveighs against the sins of drunkenness and avarice, as prologue
to the grim tale of three young rioters who set out to slay Death, whom they
find in a pile of gold, and end by slaying one another. So exalted is he by his
story that he tries to sell the pilgrims his holy relics, sheep's bones and magic
mittens, and congratulates them on having the company of one who can, for a
consideration, absolve them every mile or so as they ride along. Then,

'Peraventure there may fallen one or two
Down off his horse, and break his neck atwo.
Look what a surety is it to you alle
That I am in your fellowship y-falle,
That may absolve you, bothe more and lesse,
When that the soul shall from the body passe.
I counsel that our Host here shall beginne,
For he is most enveloped in sinne.
Come forth, Sir Host, and offer first anon,
And thou shalt kiss the relics everyone.
Yea, for a groat. Unbuckle anon thy purse.'
'Nay, nay,' quod he, 'then have I Christes curse!
Let be,' quod he, 'it shall not be, so theech!
Thou wouldest make me kiss thine olde breech
And swear it were a relic of a saint. . . .'

118

The Knight makes up the ensuing quarrel, but it may have prevented the Pardoner's being shortlisted for the free supper, though his tale of the quest for Death would have been another worthy winner.

It is now the turn of the Wife of Bath to tell a story. Plump, florid, jolly, bold, lusty, voluptuous, and most voluble of women, she cannot resist first telling her companions, with artless and engaging frankness, for there is nothing salacious in her talk, about her sexual experiences. Her first three husbands, old and rich and jealous, she tamed by accusing them of the kind of conduct that she herself practised, and flattering the doting impotents with the title of old lecher. Her fourth husband had a mistress, so she gave him real cause for jealousy: 'By God! in earth I was his purgatory.' At his funeral she fell in love with the legs of an Oxford clerk, who, though only half her age, soon became her fifth husband. Unhappily, he beat her, and so tormented her with stories about wicked wives, that one day she ripped three pages from his book. He felled her with a blow that deafened her, but she so frightened him into thinking he had killed her, that he burned his book, and ever after she had the upper hand:

> *'But, Lord Christ! when that it remembreth me*
> *Upon my youth and on my jollitee,*
> *It tickleth me about mine hearte roote.*
> *Unto this day it doth mine hearte boote*
> *That I have had my world as in my time!'*

She is now looking for a sixth husband.

The Friar laughs at this long preamble, but the Summoner tells him to shut up or amble off: a squabble that is not settled when Dame Alice resumes. Hers is a fairy-tale – for there were fairies before these wandering friars frightened them away – and a tale of Arthurian romance, though with a difference, for the moral is that wives should have the governance:

> *'And eek I pray that Jesus short their lives*
> *That will not be governed by their wives.'*

Whatever Harry Bailly's opinion may have been, posterity has unanimously awarded the prize to the self-revelations of the Wife of Bath, one of the greatest comic characters in all literature.

The quarrel between the Summoner and Friar now erupts, the Friar defining a summoner as 'a runner up and down with writs for fornication', and he tells

'I will both drink, and eaten of a cake.'
A medieval alehouse.

'A Friar there was, a wanton and a merry.
His tippet was ay farced full of knives
And pinnes, for to given faire wives.'

'A Summoner . . .
As lecherous as a sparrow.'

the story of a summoner, 'a thief and eek a bawd', who serves a forged summons on an old woman, from whom he threatens to take away her new pan if she will not pay him to withdraw his charge. 'The devil fetch him!' she cries; and the devil does, down to the region where 'summoners have their heritage'.

The infuriated Summoner then describes the nether region reserved for friars, as well as their equally unsavoury mundane activities. The hero of his tale, a begging friar, visits one of his victims, whose wife asks if he will stay to dinner:

Drinking vessel in the form of a friar, with tippet, a loose hood used as a pocket.

'Now dame,' quod he, 'now je vous dis sans doute,
Have I not of a capon but the liver,
And of your softe bread not but a shiver,
And after that a roasted pigges head –
But that I would no beast for me were dead –
Then had I with you homely suffisaunce;
I am a man of little sustenaunce.'

Chaucer's attitude towards friars, summoners and pardoners was one of amused contempt; he does not denounce or condemn, but the conclusion of *The Summoner's Tale* leaves us in little doubt of what he thought a friar worth.

The story-telling has reached another low level, and, after stopping for dinner at Sittingbourne, the Host attempts to raise the tone by asking the modest Clerk of Oxford for 'some merry thing of aventures'. The Clerk obliges with the story that he claims to have heard from Petrarch at Padua: of the outrageous humilia-

'A Clerk there was of Oxenford also,
That unto logic hadde long y-go.'

'A Merchant was ther with a forked beard
Upon his head a Flaundrish beaver hat.'

tions to which a marquis subjects his humbly-born wife Griselda, the pattern
of all patience, whose only reproach is:

> 'O goode God! how gentle and how kinde
> Ye seemed by your speech and your visage
> The day that maked was our marriage!'

The story must have tried the patience of the Wife of Bath, but then it is only
an allegory, an *exemplum*, to show how 'every wight . . . should be constant in
adversity.'

The recently married Merchant tearfully compares the ideal with the real, the
patient Griselda with his own shrewish wife, but at the Host's request tells his
tale. The matter again is marriage, but the manner a satire on courtly love: a
counterpoint of make-believe and sordid realism. All the trappings of *The
Romance of the Rose* are there: the lovely lady of fresh beauty and courtesy, a
garden 'walled all with stone', and even a well. But the 'noble knight' her
husband is an old lecher, whose slack skin shakes about his neck, and the story
a commonplace, though ingenious, one of adultery.

The Wife of Bath had begun the series of marriage tales, and as in the
Merchant's Chaucer reminds us of how she had made a purgatory of the lives
of her aged husbands, it must have been at about this time that he wrote an
*Envoy* to his friend 'Master Bukton', who was about to marry again: 'The Wife
of Bath I pray you that you reade.' The poem is a light-hearted affair, and the
line, 'Lest I myself fall eft [again] in such dotage' is a jest, and not to be taken
as an indication that his own married life with Philippa had been a failure.

'A young Squier . . .
As fresh as is the month of May.'

'A Franklin . . .
Epicurus owne son.'

'Another Nunne,
That was her chapelain.'

The pilgrims spend the night at Ospringe, ten miles from Canterbury, and next morning the Squire introduces a new theme in his artless parody of the popular romances of the period: an innocent story 'of Fairye', of magic horses, rings and mirrors, which develops so many ramifications that it threatens to go on for ever. The Franklin courteously interrupts him with congratulations, and himself tells a story that combines the former subject of marriage with the new one of magic: of vanishing rocks on the coast of Brittany. Shakespeare had it in mind when writing the famous speech of his own magician: 'Our revels now are ended . . .' for like Prospero, Chaucer's magician dissolves the vision that he has conjured up:

*clapt his handes two,*
*And farewell! all our revel was ago.*

Maison Dieu,
Ospringe, Kent.

'A man that clothed was in black;
I deemed him some Canon.'

'A gentil Manciple.'

The Franklin calls himself a 'burel', an unlettered, man, ignorant of the art of rhetoric, yet his description of a December day, the sun like copper in the frosty sky, is one of the most memorable passages in the tales, and this heartening story of constancy, compassion and generosity is another that might well have won its teller the free supper at the Tabard.

As the Nun is finishing the miraculous legend of St Cecilia, which Chaucer had written years before, the pilgrims are overtaken at the village of Boughton-under-Blean by a sweating Canon and his Yeoman, who have pursued them after having seen them leave their inn that morning: 'But it was joye for to see him sweat!' The Yeoman boasts that his master could pave the Canterbury road with gold if he so wished, but when the Host asks why he is so shabbily dressed, he whispers – but 'keep it secree' – that his professed powers of alchemy are nothing but a fraud. On seeing that his servant is betraying him, the Canon gallops off, and his Yeoman describes 'that sliding science . . . our elvish craft' and the 'sleights and infinite falseness' by which 'a canon' swindled a gullible priest out of forty pounds. It is a brilliant piece of narrative and characterization, to which Ben Jonson was probably indebted when he wrote his *Alchemist*.

The pilgrims have now reached Harbledown, not far from Canterbury – one is almost tempted to say '*we* have almost reached', so easy and intimate is Chaucer's late manner:

> *Wit ye not where there stands a little town*
> *Which that y-cleped is Bob-up-and-down,*
> *Under the Blee in Caunterbury Waye?*

123

'A good man was ther of religioun,
That was a poore Parson of a town.'

The Cook is yawning and nodding in the rear, and the Host calls 'Hast thou had fleas all night, or art thou drunk?' He is so drunk that when the Manciple mocks him, he falls off his horse in speechless fury, leaving the Manciple to recount Ovid's story of how the crow became black.

It is four o'clock as the Host turns to the Parson, 'For every man, save thou, hath told his tale.' It is true that most of the pilgrims have told one tale, but they are still less than a quarter of the way through their total of four stories each. 'Thou gettest fable none y-told for me,' the good Parson replies severely:

> *I am a Southren man,*
> *I cannot geste* rum, ram, ruf, *by lettre,*
> *Ne, God wot, rhyme hold I but little bettre.*

He is not one of your northern writers of alliterative romance, nor one of your new-fangled rhymers of fables, but he will tell 'a merry tale in prose'.

The Parson's merry tale is a sermon on the Seven Deadly Sins and the proper preparation for the last 'glorious pilgrimage' to the heavenly Jerusalem. He is outspoken, particularly on the sin of Pride, as manifested in the extrava-gant dress of Chaucer's time, both in its superfluity and 'horrible disordinate scantness': the long gowns 'trailing in the dung and in the mire', the short jackets that reveal men's buttocks 'as it were the hinder part of a she-ape in the full of the moon'.

The sun is setting as the Parson concludes his sermon, and the pilgrims ride into Canterbury. What happened there we shall never know. Chaucer was

124

The West Gate through which the Pilgrims entered Canterbury. It had just been completed. ▶

# CANTERBVRY.

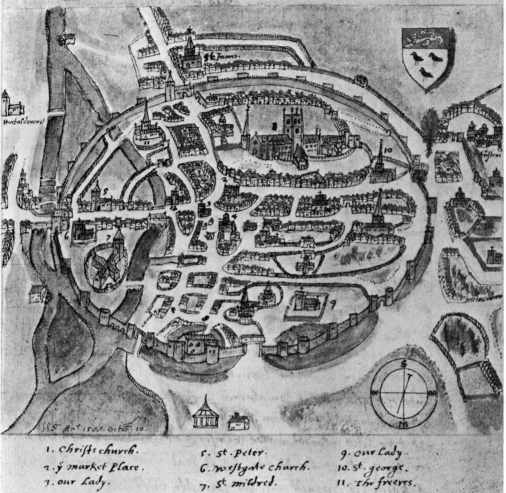

1. Chrifts church.
2. ỳ market place.
3. our Lady.
4. st Andrewes.

5. st peter.
6. weftgate church.
7. st mildred.
8. the caftell.

9. our Lady.
10. st george.
11. the freeres.
12. Afhalows.

◀ 'Till that we come to Caunterbury town.'

Second Common seal of the City of Canterbury showing the martyrdom of Thomas à Becket.

nearing the end of his own sixty-year pilgrimage and, like a devout son of the Catholic Church, asked pardon for anything he had written 'of worldly vanities', from *The Book of the Duchess* to the *Tales of Canterbury*, 'the which I revoke in my retractions.' And may 'our Lord Jesus Christ . . . from henceforth unto my life's end, send me grace to bewail my guilts, and to study to the salvation of my soul.'

He had not much longer to go. He died towards the end of the last year of the fourteenth century, on 25 October 1400, and was buried, almost within his garden, in the south transept of Westminster Abbey, first of the company of pilgrims who were to assemble in Poets' Corner.

'Master Geffray Chaucer, that now lyth in grave,
The nobyll rethoricien, and poet of Great Bretayne.'

# A SHORT BIBLIOGRAPHY

WORKS

*The Complete Works of Geoffrey Chaucer.* Ed. W. W. Skeat, 7 vols, 1894–7.
*The Works of Geoffrey Chaucer.* Ed. F. N. Robinson, 1 vol., 1933.
*Chaucer's Poetry: an anthology for the modern reader.* E. T. Donaldson, 1958.
*The Canterbury Tales,* translated into modern verse by N. Coghill, 1951.
*The Prologue to the Canterbury Tales and The Nun's Priest's Tale,* read in Middle English by N. Coghill, N. Davis and J. Burrow, 1964, 1966. Argo Record Co. RG 401, 466.


LIFE AND CRITICISM

*A Chaucer Handbook.* R. D. French, 1947.
*Chaucer Life-Records.* Ed. M. M. Crow and C. C. Olson, 1966.
*Geoffrey Chaucer of England.* M. Chute, 1951.
*Five Hundred Years of Chaucer. Criticism and Allusion.* C. F. E. Spurgeon, 1925.
*Chaucer.* G. K. Chesterton, 1932.
*Geoffrey Chaucer.* J. L. Lowes, 1934.
*Chaucer and his Poetry.* G. L. Kittredge, 1946.
*Chaucer's Early Poetry.* W. Clemen, 1964.
*The Poet Chaucer.* N. Coghill, 1967.


BACKGROUND

*England in the Age of Wycliffe.* G. M. Trevelyan, 1899.
*English Wayfaring Life in the Middle Ages.* J. J. Jusserand, 1899.
*Chaucer and His England.* G. G. Coulton, 1930.
*Chaucer's World.* (Illustrated). E. Rickert, 1948.
*England in the Late Middle Ages.* A. R. Myers, 1952.
*A Mirror of Chaucer's World* (Illustrated). R. S. Loomis, 1966.
*The Flowering of the Middle Ages* (Illustrated). Ed. J. Evans, 1966.
*Chaucer's World: a Pictorial Companion.* M. Hussey, 1967.

# CHRONOLOGY

1327  Accession of Edward III, aged fourteen.

1338  Beginning of the Hundred Years War.

c. 1340  Geoffrey Chaucer born in London, the son of John Chaucer, vintner, and his wife Agnes de Copton.

1348–9  The Black Death.

1357  A page in the service of Prince Lionel, Earl of Ulster, and his Countess. Probably meets Lionel's younger brother, John of Gaunt.

1359  Taken prisoner near Rheims, when on a campaign with the King and Prince Lionel.

1360  March. Edward III contributes £16 towards his ransom.
Carries letters between Calais and London.

c. 1363  Enters the service of Edward III.

c. 1366  John Chaucer, his father, dies.
Marries Philippa de Roet, a lady-in-waiting to Queen Philippa, from whom she receives the first payment of an annuity of 10 marks.

1367  Edward III grants his 'beloved valet' Geoffrey Chaucer an annuity of 20 marks.
Translating *The Romaunt of the Rose*. (?)

1368  Now an esquire of the King, he is sent on a mission abroad.

1369  A plague year. Death of Queen Philippa and of John of Gaunt's first wife, Blanche, Duchess of Lancaster. Military service in France, probably with John of Gaunt.
*The Book of the Duchess.*

1370  June–September. A mission abroad.

1372  John of Gaunt marries Constance of Castile; Philippa Chaucer becomes her lady-in-waiting and receives first payment of an annuity of £10.
1 December. Starts on his first visit to Italy: to Genoa, Florence and possibly Padua.

1373  May. Returns from Italy.
Sent to Dartmouth to investigate the complaint of a Genoese sea-captain.

1374  23 April. The King awards him a daily pitcher of wine.
10 May. The London Corporation lease him the house above Aldgate, rent-free.
2 June. Appointed Controller of Customs and Subsidy of Wools, Skins and Hides, with salary of £10.
13 June. John of Gaunt gives him a pension of £10 for life.

1375  Given wardship of two Kentish boys: Edward Staplegate and William de Solys.

c. 1376  The Black Prince dies.
Sent to France on secret negotiations.
*The Life of St Cecilia* and *The House of Fame*. (?)

1377  Two diplomatic missions to France: February–March, and May–June.
21 June. Edward III dies and is succeeded by the Black Prince's son, the ten-year-old Richard II.
Chaucer confirmed in his office of Controller.

1378  January. Attends abortive peace negotiations in France.
March. Confirmation of Edward III's annuity of 20 marks.
April. Commutes his daily pitcher of wine for an annual payment of 20 marks.
May–September. Second visit to Italy, with Sir Edward Berkeley, to negotiate

with Bernabo Visconti of Milan, probably for a war-loan.

1380 Cecily Chaumpaigne releases Chaucer of all her rights of action 'tam de raptu meo'.
*Anelida and Arcite.* (?)

1381 June. The Peasants' Revolt. Chaucer sells his property in Thames Street.
His son Lewis born. (?)
*The Parliament of Fowls.* (?)

1382 Richard II marries Princess Anne of Bohemia.
May. Chaucer appointed Controller of Petty Customs in addition to that of Wools.
Translates *Boethius.* (?)

c. 1383-5 *Troilus and Criseyde.*

1383-4 Allowed to appoint a deputy at the Wool Customs for five months, because of his own affairs.

1385 February. Allowed to appoint a permanent deputy at the Wool Quay.
Moves into Kent (?) probably Greenwich.
*The Legend of Good Women.* (?)
October. A Justice of the Peace for Kent.

1386 October. Returned to Parliament as one of the Knights of the Shire for Kent.
John of Gaunt abroad, and ascendancy of Duke of Gloucester.
A witness in the case of Scrope *v* Grosvenor.
Gives up his Aldgate house.
December. Either resigns or is dismissed from his Controllerships.
*Fortune: Ballades de Visage sanz Peinture.* (?)

1387 April. Begins *The Canterbury Tales.* (?)
July. With Sir William Beauchamp to Calais: his last foreign mission.
Death of his wife Philippa.

1388 Raises money by selling his two royal annuities of 20 marks each.

1389 Richard asserts his authority, and John of Gaunt returns to England.
July. Chaucer appointed Clerk of the King's Works.

1390 March. One of a Commission to survey the banks of the Thames.
Ordered to superintend repair of St George's Chapel, Windsor.
September. Robbed three times by highwaymen.

1391 June. Resigns Clerkship of the Works to become Deputy Forester of North Petherton.
*A Treatise on the Astrolabe.*

1393 *The Envoy of Chaucer to Scogan.* (?)
Gift of £10 in return for 'good service to the King'.

1394 February. Richard II grants Chaucer an annuity of £20.

1396 John of Gaunt marries Chaucer's sister-in-law, Katherine Swynford.

1398 Sued for a debt of £14 by Isabella Buckholt.

1399 John of Gaunt dies, and Richard II seizes his estates.
September. Richard II abdicates, and John of Gaunt's son becomes King Henry IV.
*The Complaint of Chaucer to his Purse* addressed to the new King.
3 October. Henry IV confirms Richard II's annuity of £20 and adds another of 40 marks.
24 December. Takes a 53-year lease of a house in the garden of Westminster Abbey.

1400 5 June. Last recorded payment of his annuity. 25 October, dies. Buried in Westminster Abbey.

# GLOSSARY

Aller: of all
Anon: at once

Boote: good
Brenning: burning

Can: know
Clepen: call, name

Deliverly: quickly
Drasty: worthless
Dure: endure

Eek: also
Eem: uncle

Ferly: marvel
Flour: flower

Geste: tell a story
Glose: comment, excuse
Grant mercy: many thanks
Groat: fourpence

Hente: seized
Hight: was called

Laton: brass
Lewed: ignorant
Lite, Lyte: little

Make: mate
Meede: mead, meadow
Meven: move, happen
Meynee: company, mob

Noot: know not

Paindemain: white bread
Poppet: puppet, doll
Purvey: provide, prepare

Quod: quoth, said

Rape: haste
Reede: red

Shend: harm, ruin
Sireyns: sirens
Soote, swote: sweet
Stark: strong
Stint: stopped
Strake: return home
Sweven: dream
Swyve: play the harlot

Teen: grief, vexation
Theech: may I thrive
Thilke: the same
Tho: then

Wight: person, man
Woon: plenty
Wot: know
Wrythen: wriggle

Yard: garden
Yerne: quickly
Y-frounced: wrinkled
Y-grave: dug up, cut
Yore: long
Y-wis: certainly

The Ellesmere manuscript of Chaucer's *Canterbury Tales* is now in the Henry E. Huntington Library, San Marino, California, USA. The manuscript is dated 1400–10, though the miniatures are later. The illustrations reproduced in this book have been taken from a facsimile of the original manuscript

*Frontispiece.* PORTRAIT OF CHAUCER, from a copy of *De Regimine Principum* by Thomas Hoccleve. English. Early 15th century. B.M. MS. Roy. 17 D. VI f. 93v

7 AGAS map of London, detail. *c.* 1560–70. From the facsimile in the British Museum of the copies in the Guildhall Library, London and Magdalene College, Cambridge

8 VINTAGE MISERICORD. Gloucester Cathedral. 14th century. *Photo Edwin Smith*

DEED, witnessed by John Chaucer, whereby Edmund de Sutton granted John de Stodeye the vintry estates in London, 12 April 1352. *Photo Brompton Studio*

9 WINE TRADERS at the port of Paris, from *La Vie de St Denis.* French. 1317. MS. Fr. 2091 f. 125. Bibliothèque Nationale, Paris

SIXTH SEAL of Edward III. *c.* 1350. B.M., London

10 MAYORALTY of the Wool Staple, Westminster. Seal die. Probably 1393. B.M., London

SHEEP-SHEARING, from an *Hours of the Virgin.* Flemish. Late 15th century. B.M. MS. Add. 17012 f. 6r

LONDON BRIDGE. Detail from the panoramic view of London by Anthony van der Wyngaerde. 1543. From the facsimile of the drawing in the Ashmolean Museum, Oxford

11 SOUTH BANK of the Thames with St Mary Overie. Detail from the panoramic view of London by Anthony van der Wyngaerde. 1543. From the facsimile of the drawing in the Ashmolean Museum, Oxford

12 COURT OF THE KING'S BENCH. One of four miniatures on vellum extracted from a book of law terms depicting the superior courts at Westminster. *c.* 1460. Library of the Inner Temple, London. By permission of the Treasurer and Masters of the Bench of the Inner Temple

13 GUILD MASTER with a carpenter and a mason, from *Des Proprietez des Choses.* Flemish. Late 15th century. B.M. MS. Roy. 15 E.2 f. 265

14 MARGINAL ILLUMINATION from the Beatus page of the *Gorleston Psalter.* English. *c.* 1310–25. B.M. MS. Add. 49622 f. 8

15 NORTH FACE of the Percy Shrine. Beverley Minster, Yorkshire. Mid 14th century. *Photo: National Monuments Record*

16 SCENES OF COURTLY LOVE. Ivory panel from a boxwood casket. French. 14th century. Gambier-Parry Collection, Courtauld Institute Galleries, London.

TRISTAN AND ISOLDE at the fountain and asleep with the sword between them. Ivory panel from the 'Tristan Casket'. French. Mid 14th century. The Hermitage, Leningrad. *Photo: Society for Cultural Relations with the USSR*

17 A TOURNAMENT and storming the Castle of Love. Ivory lid of a casket. French. 14th century. City of Liverpool Museums

18 PINK WARE JUG with fleur-de-lis applied in red clay. English, 14th century. B.M. London

GOLD NOBLE of Edward III, struck between 1360 and 1369. B.M., London

SIR GEOFFREY LUTTRELL of Irnham mounted, attended by his wife, Agnes Sutton and daughter-in-law, Beatrice Scrope, from the *Luttrell Psalter*. East Anglian. *c.* 1335–40. B.M. MS. Add. 42130 f. 202v

19 EDWARD III in robes of the Order of the Garter. Tinted drawing by Sir William Bruges (*d.* 1449), first Garter King of Arms. English. Early 15th century. B.M. MS. Stowe 594 f. 7v

20 BURNING INFECTED CLOTHES during the Black Death, from a copy of *The Romance of Alexander* by Lambert di Tours and Alexandre de Bernay. French manuscript illuminated at Bruges. 1338–44. MS. Bod. 264 f. 83r. Bodleian Library, Oxford

RIOTERS pillaging a house, from the *Chroniques de France ou de Saint Denis*. French. Late 14th century. B.M. MS. Roy. 20 C. VII f. 41v

ARCHERY SCENE, from the *Luttrell Psalter*. East Anglian. *c.* 1335–40. B.M. MS. Add. 42130 f. 147v

21 BATTLE SCENE, from the Holkham Bible Picture Book. English. *c.* 1327–35. B.M. MS. Add. 47682 f. 40

22 PART OF THE ULSTER HOUSEHOLD ACCOUNTS. 1357. B.M. MS. Add. 18632 f. 101v

23 WINDSOR CASTLE. Drawing by Wenceslaus Hollar (1607–77). Royal Library, Windsor Castle. Reproduced by gracious permission of Her Majesty the Queen

24 PAGE helping his lord to dress. 'February' miniature from the *Queen Mary Psalter*. English. Early 14th century. B.M. MS. Roy. 2 B. VII f. 72v

KNIGHTS riding to a tournament, from the *Chroniques de France et d'Angleterre* by Jehan Froissart. Flemish. c. 1460–80. B.M. MS. Harley 4379 f. 99

25 PAGE attending table. 'January' miniature from the *Queen Mary Psalter*. English. Early 14th century. B.M. MS. Roy. 2 B VII f. 71v

A BAGPIPER. Stone label stop (partly restored). Beverley Minster, Yorkshire. *c.* 1320–30. *Photo: National Monuments Record*

HAWKING PARTY. Tinted drawing from the *Queen Mary Psalter*. English. Early 14th century. B.M. MS. Roy. 2 B. VII f. 151

27 BATTLE OF POITIERS, from the *St Albans Chronicle*. Flemish. 15th century. MS. 6 E.2 f. 22 iv. Lambeth Palace Library

AERIAL VIEW of Restormel Castle, Cornwall. Late 13th century. *Photo copyright: Country Life*

28 LIONEL, DUKE OF CLARENCE. Gilt copper weeper on the tomb of Edward III *c.* 1377–80. Westminster Abbey, London. *Photo: Royal Commission on Historical Monuments. (Crown copyright)*

IMPRISONMENT OF JOHN OF FRANCE, from *Des cas des nobles hommes et femmes maleureux*. Flemish translation of Boccaccio. 1470–83. B.M. MS. Roy. 14 E. V f. 510

EDWARD III giving his son, the Prince of Wales, the grant of the principality of Aquitaine. Miniature from a copy of the grant. 1362. B.M. MS. Cotton Nero D. 6 f. 31

29 RHEIMS CATHEDRAL. The west front 1254–90; towers completed by 1427. *Photo: Martin Hürlimann*

30 CHART OF HARBOUR and road of Calais. English. 16th century. B.M. MS. Cotton Augustus I ii 70

EDWARD III's annuity to Chaucer, 1367. Chancery Patent Rolls 66, 41 Ed. III, Pt. I, m. 13. Public Record Office

31 GILT AND PAINTED PARADE SHIELD. Flemish. Late 15th century. B.M., London

32 THE DREAMING POET, from a copy of the *Roman de la Rose*. French. 15th century. B.M. MS. Egerton 1069 f. 1

33 MEDIEVAL WALLED GARDEN, from a copy of the *Roman de la Rose*. Flemish. Late 15th century. B.M. MS. Harley 4425 f. 12v

34 THE CAPTURE of Pedro the Cruel, from a *Life of Bertrand Duguesclin* by Jean Cuvelier. French. *c.* 1390. B.M. MS. Yates Thompson 35 f. 246

35 PORTRAIT OF CHAUCER, from a copy of *De Regimine Principum* by Thomas Hoc‑cleve. English. *c.* 1410. B.M. MS. Harley 4866 f. 88

36 PHILIPPA OF HAINAULT. White marble effigy by Jean de Liège. Flemish. *c.* 1365–7. Westminster Abbey, London. *Photo: By permission of the Dean and Chapter of Westminster*

37 TOMB OF JOHN OF GAUNT and his wife, Blanche of Lancaster. Alabaster. *c.* 1374. Engraving from W. Dugdale's *The History of St Paul's Cathedral*, 1716

38 THE LOVE‑SICK POET and Alcione kneel‑ing before Juno with the body of Ceyx drowned in the sea, from Machaut's *Dit de la Fontaine Amoureuse*. French. *c.* 1370. MS. Fr. 1584 f. 157v. Bibliothèque Nationale, Paris

39 RICHMOND CASTLE, from the *Register of the Honour of Richmond*, Yorkshire. English. *c.* 1410. MS. Lyell 22 f. 21v. Bodleian Library, Oxford

40–1 HART‑HUNTING SCENE. Ivory panel. French. 14th century. Collection Waller‑stein‑Oettingen, Maihingen. *Photo: Ar‑chives Photographiques*

41 A GAME OF CHESS. Ivory mirror‑case. French. 14th century. Victoria and Albert Museum, London

42 THE ARMS OF JOHN OF GAUNT. Stained glass panel. English. Late 14th century. Victoria and Albert Museum, London

42–3 THE SAVOY. Drawing by Wenceslaus Hollar (1607–77). Pepysian Library. By permission of the Master and Fellows of Magdalene College, Cambridge

43 PORTRAIT OF JOHN OF GAUNT, from the *Donation Book of Benefactors of St Albans Abbey*. English. *c.* 1380. B.M. MS. Cotton Nero D. VII f. 7

45 ROSE WINDOW of the Cathedral of Notre‑Dame d'Evreux. 1511–31. *Photo: Martin Hürlimann*
GREAT EAST WINDOW of Gloucester Cathe‑dral. 1347–50. *Photo: Martin Hürlimann*

47 MINIATURE from the manuscript of *Piers Plowman* by William Langland. MS. CCC. 201 f. 1r. Corpus Christi College, Oxford. By courtesy of the President and Fellows of Corpus Christi College
ILLUSTRATION FROM a copy of *Pearl*. English. 14th century. B.M. MS. Cotton Nero A.X. f. 42v
ILLUSTRATION FROM *Sir Gawain and the Green Knight*. English. 14th century. B.M. MS. Cotton Nero A.X. f. 129v

48 EFFIGY OF JOHN GOWER (*d.* 1408). Southwark Cathedral, London. *Photo: Royal Commission on Historical Monuments. (Crown copyright)*

49 PORTRAIT OF DANTE AND PETRARCH by Giovanni dal Ponte. Florentine. 15th century. Courtesy of the Fogg Art Museum, Harvard University. Gift of the Society of Friends of the Fogg Art Museum

50 VIEW OF GENOA, from Hartmann Schedel's *Liber Chronicarum*, 1493

50–1 GENOESE MONEYLENDERS, from *De septem vitiis*. Italian. Late 14th century. B.M. MS. Add. 27695 f. 7v
GOOD GOVERNMENT IN THE COUNTRY. Fresco by Ambrogio Lorenzetti. *c.* 1337–9. Palazzo Pubblico, Siena. *Photo: Grassi*

51 JUSTICE. Fresco by Giotto in the Scrovegni Chapel, Padua. 1303–5. *Photo: The Mansell Collection*
VIEW OF FLORENCE. Detail from the fresco of the *Misericordia*. 1352. Bigallo, Florence. *Photo: The Mansell Collection*

52 SCENES FROM THE *Decameron*. Panels from a marriage chest attributed to Rossello di Jacopo Franchi. *c.* 1420–30. National Gallery of Scotland, Edinburgh

53 CHART OF DARTMOUTH HARBOUR. Eng‑lish. 16th century. B.M. MS. Cotton Augustus I i 39

54 CHAUCER'S SEAL, used by Thomas Chaucer in 1409. Document E. 212/79. Public Record Office, London
SEAL OF THE DELIVERY OF WOOLS and hides at Winchester and seal of the Port of London. Probably the reign of Edward I. B.M., London

55 HOUSE OF FAME woodcut, from an edition of Chaucer's works, printed by Richard Pynson, 1526

57 A ZODIAC MAN, from the *Très Riches Heures* of the Duke of Berry, illuminated by the Limbourg brothers. 15th century. Musée Condé, Chantilly. *Photo: Giraudon*

58 BODIAM CASTLE, Sussex. 1386. *Photo: Aerofilms Ltd*

59 ADAM AND EVE, from a Latin *Pentateuch*. English. Early 14th century. B.M. MS. Roy. 1 E. IV f. 12v

MARTYRDOM OF ST CECILIA, from the Altarpiece of Sta Cecilia by an unknown master. Italian. 14th century. Uffizi, Florence. *Photo: The Mansell Collection*

60 THE PAPAL PALACE, Avignon. 1316–64. (Watchtowers are modern additions.) *Photo: Jean Roubier*

61 FLEMISH WEAVERS' cottages, Lavenham, Suffolk. 14th century. *Photo: Library of the Central Office of Information, London. (Crown copyright)*

TITHE BARN, Bradford-on-Avon, Wiltshire. 14th century. *Photo: A. F. Kersting*

62 THE BLACK PRINCE. Gilt copper effigy. *c.* 1377–80. Canterbury Cathedral. *Photo: National Monuments Record*

63 WILLIAM OF WYKEHAM. Alabaster effigy. *c.* 1399–1403. Winchester Cathedral. *Photo: Royal Commission on Historical Monuments. (Crown copyright)*

64 PLAN OF PARIS, from Sebastian Münster's *Cosmographia Universalis*, 1550

ILE DE LA CITE, Paris. Detail from the miniature of the *Descent of the Holy Ghost* by Jean Fouquet. Mid 15th century. The Lehman Collection, New York

65 EDWARD III. Gilt copper effigy. *c.* 1377–80. Westminster Abbey, London. *Photo: Royal Commission on Historical Monuments. (Crown copyright)*

RICHARD II holding court, from the *Chroniques d'Angleterre* by Jean de Wavrin. Flemish. Late 15th century. B.M. MS. Roy. 14 E. IV f. 10

66 MONUMENT TO BERNABO VISCONTI (*d.* 1385) by Bonino da Campione. Castello Sforzesco, Milan. *Photo: The Mansell Collection*

67 SIR JOHN HAWKWOOD. Fresco by Paolo Uccello. 1436. Florence Cathedral. *Photo: The Mansell Collection*

68 PORTRAIT OF SIR JOHN PHILIPOT, from the *Donation Book of Benefactors of St Albans Abbey*. English. *c.* 1380. B.M. MS. Cotton Nero D. VII f. 105v

69 PEACOCK AND OTHER BIRDS, from a sketch-book by divers hands. English. *c.* 1400. MS. 1916 f. 13r. Pepysian Library. By permission of the Master and Fellows of Magdalene College, Cambridge

71 THE PEASANTS' REVOLT, from the *Chroniques de France et d'Angleterre* by Jehan Froissart. Flemish. *c.* 1460–80. B.M. MS. Roy. 18 E. 1 f. 175

THE TOWER OF LONDON, from a copy of the *Poems of Charles, Duke of Orleans*. Probably executed in England in the Flemish style, *c.* 1500. B.M. MS. Roy. 16 F.2 f. 73

72 TWO SEALS for labourers' passes under the Statute of Cambridge, 1388. B.M., London

73 THE WHEEL OF FORTUNE, from the Holkham Bible Picture Book. English. *c.* 1327–35. B.M. MS. Add. 47682 f. 1v

PAGE FROM THE WYCLIFFE BIBLE. English. Late 14th century. B.M. MS. Egerton 618 f. 74

74 TROILUS AND CRISEYDE, from the *Liber de casu et ruina Trojae* by Guidonis de Columnis. Italian. Mid 14th century. B.M. MS. Add. 15477 f. 35v

75 LYDGATE presenting his poem, *The Pilgrim*, to Thomas Montacute, Earl of Salisbury. English. 15th century. B.M. MS. Harley 4826, frontispiece

CHAUCER reading to a noble company, from a copy of *Troilus and Criseyde*. English. *c.* 1400. Corpus Christi College, Cambridge. By permission of the Master and Fellows. MS. 61, frontispiece

77 BOETHIUS in his library, from a copy of

*De consolatione Philosophiae.* Flemish. 1476. B.M. MS. Harley 4335 f. 1r

78 A SCRIBE, from Bede's *Life of St Cuthbert.* English. Late 12th century. B.M. MS. Add. 39943 f. 2

MERTON COLLEGE, OXFORD. Engraving from David Loggan's *Oxonia Illustrata,* 1675

79 GREENWICH, from the panoramic view of London by Anthony van der Wyngaerde. 1543. From the facsimile of the drawing in the Ashmolean Museum, Oxford

80 WOMEN PICKING DAISIES. 'April' minia-ture from the *Queen Mary Psalter.* English. Early 14th century. B.M. MS. Roy. 2 B. VII f. 74 v

81 PORTRAIT OF CHAUCER, with a daisy motif and his coat of arms. English. Late 16th century. B.M. MS. Add. 5141 f.1

83 THE MONTH OF MAY, from the *Très Riches Heures* of the Duke of Berry by the Lim-bourg brothers. 15th century. Musée Condé, Chantilly. *Photo: Giraudon*

84-5 ELTHAM PALACE. Engraving from Buck's *Antiquities,* vol. I, 1774

85 THE GREAT HALL, Penshurst Place. 14th century. *Photo: A. F. Kersting*

86-7 NAVAL BATTLE from a history of the world. French manuscript illuminated in Italy. 14th century. B.M. MS. Roy. 20 D. 1 f. 258

89 PARLIAMENT sitting at Westminster, from *Histoire du Roy d'Angleterre Richard II* by Jehan Creton. French. Early 15th century. B.M. MS. Harley 1319 f. 57

KING OF PORTUGAL entertaining John of Gaunt, from the *Chronique d'Angleterre* by Jean de Wavrin. Flemish. Late 15th century. B.M. MS. Roy. 14 E. IV f. 244v

90 PILGRIM BADGE of St Thomas. 14th 15th century. B.M., London

90-1 VIEW OF ROME, from Hartmann Schedel's *Liber Chronicarum,* 1493

91 THE GOUGH MAP of the British Isles. Detail of the south-east of England. *c.* 1360. Bodleian Library, Oxford

CHURCH OF THE HOLY SEPULCHRE,

Jerusalem, from the *Hours of René of Anjou.* French. 1436. B.M. MS. Egerton 1070 f. 5r

92 READING A FABRICATED PAPAL BULL in Canterbury Cathedral, from the *Histoire du Roy d'Angleterre Richard II* by Jehan Creton. French. Early 15th century. B.M. MS. Harley 1319 f. 12r

93 NAVE OF CANTERBURY CATHEDRAL. Begun 1378. *Photo: Martin Hürlimann*

94 ROUTE FROM LONDON TO DOVER. Section of an itinerary from London to Jerusalem in *Historia Anglorum* by Matthew Paris. English 1250-59. B.M. MS. Roy. 14 C. VII f. 2

NUN AND FRIAR in the stocks, from the *Smithfield Decretals.* Written in Italy and illuminated in England. Early 14th cen-tury. B.M. MS. Roy. 10 E. IV. f. 187r

MAKING BEDS at an inn, from the *Pilgrim-age of the Life of Man,* Lydgate's translation of G. de Deguileville's work. English. Early 15th century. B.M. MS. Cotton Tiberius X.A. vii f. 90

95 PILGRIMS ON THE ROAD, from Lydgate's *Troy Book and the Story of Thebes.* Miniature in Flemish style. 16th century. B.M. MS. Roy. 18 D. 2 f. 148

97 THE SHRINE OF ST THOMAS. Detail from window V in the Chapel of St Thomas, Canterbury Cathedral. *c.* 1220. *Photo: Victoria and Albert Museum, London*

THE MARTYRDOM of Thomas à Becket, from a *Psalter* from Romsey Abbey. East Anglian. *c.* 1300. MS. 302 f. 8. Pierpont Morgan Library, New York

98-9 THE CANTERBURY PILGRIMS. Engraving by William Blake after his fresco. 1810. B.M., London

99 AN ASTROLOGER observing the heavens, from an encyclopaedia, *Omne Bonum.* English. Mid 14th century. B.M. MS. Roy. 6 E. VI f. 396v

PILGRIMS AT SUPPER, from Wynkyn de Worde's edition of *The Canterbury Tales,* 1498

101 A ROBBER'S ATTACK, from *La estoire de*

*Seint Aedward le Rei.* English. Mid 13th century. MS. Ee. 3.59. f 4r. Cambridge University Library

102 WESTMINSTER HALL, London. Timber roof designed by Yevele and built 1395–6. *Photo: A. F. Kersting*

103 A TOURNAMENT, from *Histoire du Petit Jehan de Saintre.* French. 15th century. B.M. MS. Cotton Nero D. IX f. 32v
PORCH of the cloister of St George's Chapel, Windsor Castle. *c.* 1350. *Photo: G. Spearman.* Reproduced by courtesy of the Hon. Editors of the Annual Report of the Friends of St George's Chapel

104 THE SLOANE ASTROLABE. English. *c.* 1280. B.M., London

105 FORESTERS AT WORK, from a Spanish *Breviary.* Flemish miniature. Late 15th century. B.M. MS. Add. 18851 f. 2

107 THOMAS CHAUCER and his wife, Maud. Brass on the altar tomb. Church of St Mary, Ewelme. *Photo: Royal Commission on Historical Monuments.* (*Crown copyright*)
LEASE from the Warden of the Lady Chapel, Westminster, to Chaucer of a tenement in the garden of the Chapel for 53 years. 1399. Reproduced by permission of the Dean and Chapter of Westminster

108 RICHARD II and his wife, Anne of Bohemia. Gilt copper effigy by Nicholas Broker and Godfrey Prest. 1394–6. Westminster Abbey, London. *Photo: A. F. Kersting*
ABDICATION OF RICHARD II, from the *Chroniques de France et d'Angleterre* by Jehan Froissart. Flemish. *c.* 1460–80. B.M. MS. Harley 4380 f. 184v

109 CORONATION OF HENRY IV, from the *Chroniques de France et d'Angleterre* by Jehan Froissart. Flemish. *c.* 1460–80. B.M. MS. Harley 4380 f. 186v

110 FIRST PAGE of the Prologue to *The Canterbury Tales.* Ellesmere manuscript f. 5r

111 THE KNIGHT. Ellesmere manuscript f. 14r
THE MILLER. Ellesmere manuscript f. 38v
THE REEVE. Ellesmere manuscript f. 46r

112 THE COOK. Ellesmere manuscript f. 51r

VARIOUS PILGRIM BADGES. 14th–15th century. B.M., London

113 THE MAN OF LAW. Ellesmere manuscript f. 54v
THE SHIPMAN. Ellesmere manuscript f. 147v
THE PRIORESS. Ellesmere manuscript f. 152v

114 PORTRAIT OF CHAUCER. Ellesmere manuscript f. 157v

115 THE MONK. Ellesmere manuscript f. 173r

116 THE NUN'S PRIEST. Ellesmere manuscript f. 183r
THE PHYSICIAN. Ellesmere manuscript f. 137r
A PHYSICIAN. Marginal drawing from John of Gaddesden's *Rosa Medicina (Anglica).* Exeter Cathedral Library. By permission of the Dean and Chapter of Exeter Cathedral

117 SEAL OF THE CITY OF ROCHESTER, showing the castle. 13th century. B.M., London. *Photo: Courtauld Institute of Art*
PLAN OF THE CITY OF ROCHESTER, from *A Description of England,* 1588. B.M. MS. Sloane 2596 f. 16

118 THE PARDONER. Ellesmere manuscript f. 142r
THE WIFE OF BATH. Ellesmere manuscript f. 76r

119 AN ALEHOUSE, from the *Smithfield Decretals.* Written in Italy and illuminated in England. Early 14th century. B.M. MS. Roy. 10 E. IV f. 114v
DRINKING VESSEL in the form of a friar with a tippet, hood and sack-like cloak, holding a book. English. Early 15th century. B.M., London

120 THE FRIAR. Ellesmere manuscript f. 80v
THE SUMMONER. Ellesmere manuscript f. 85r

121 THE CLERK OF OXFORD. Ellesmere manuscript f. 92r
THE MERCHANT. Ellesmere manuscript f. 106v

122 THE SQUIRE. Ellesmere manuscript f. 119v
THE FRANKLIN. Ellesmere manuscript f. 127v

THE NUN. Ellesmere manuscript f. 191r

MAISON DIEU, Ospringe. House incorporating an original undercroft of a subsidiary building of the hospital of Blessed Mary at Ospringe, founded early 13th century. *Photo: Royal Commission on Historical Monuments. (Crown copyright)*

123 THE CANON'S YEOMAN. Ellesmere manuscript f. 198r

THE MANCIPLE. Ellesmere manuscript f. 207r

124 THE PARSON. Ellesmere manuscript f. 210v

125 THE WEST GATE, Canterbury. *Photo: Walter Scott*

126 PILGRIMS mounted and on foot. Detail from window III in the Chapel of St Thomas, Canterbury Cathedral. *c.* 1220. *Photo: Victoria and Albert Museum, London*

127 PLAN OF THE CITY OF CANTERBURY, from *A Description of England*, 1588. B.M. MS. Sloan 2596 f. 15

SECOND COMMON SEAL of the city of Canterbury, showing the martyrdom of Thomas à Becket. 1357. B.M., London

128 TOMB OF CHAUCER, erected by Nicolas Brigham. 1556. Westminster Abbey, London. *Photo: National Monuments Record*